W9-ALT-684

Soldiers from the Ghetto

Soldiers from the Ghetto

Shalom Cholawski

SAN DIEGO • NEW YORK
A. S. BARNES & COMPANY, INC.
IN LONDON:
THE TANTIVY PRESS
New York: The Herzl Press

©1980 by A.S. Barnes and Co., Inc.

A. S. Barnes & Co., Inc.
11175 Flintkote Ave.
San Diego, CA 92121

Tantivy Press
Magdalen House
136-148 Tooley Street
London SE1 2TT, England

Library of Congress Cataloging in Publication Data

Cholawski, Shalom.
Soldiers from the ghetto.

1. Jews in Nesvizh, Byelorussian S. S. R.--Persecutions.
2. Holocaust, Jewish (1939-1945)--White Russia--Nesvizh--
Personal narratives. 3. World War, 1939-1945--Underground
movements--Jews. 4. Cholawski, Shalom. 5. Nesvizh,
Byelorussian S. S. R.--Ethnic relations.
I. Title.
DS135.R93N453   940.53 '1503 '9240947652   78-75300
ISBN 0-498-02382-6

Printed in the United States of America

Foreword

Shalom Cholawski's book is an important contribution to the growing literature of the Holocaust. It is both a personal memoir and a well-researched piece of historical writing. To those who know Shalom Cholawski's writings — all of them in Hebrew — this does not come as a surprise. His editing of the *Sefer Hapartizanim* (Book of the Partisans) in the fifties was the first step in chronicling Jewish armed resistance in the forests of Eastern Europe and a fitting prelude to his present preoccupation. His description of the rebellion of the Jews of Tuczyn, in the Hebrew publication *Yalkut Moreshet* (which he helped found and on whose editorial board he is still active) was another step. The present little volume goes even further. Cholawski was the commander of the first ghetto rebellion to take place anywhere in Europe, and by a miracle he lived to tell the story — all those who lived to tell the story survived by a miracle. The fact that in addition to being witness, participant and main actor in the story he describes he is also an academically trained historian gives added value to this significant testimony.

Nesvizh was one of the hundreds of Jewish *shtetls* in Eastern Poland and Western Belorussia and Ukraine; like all *shtetls*, it was different from all the other *shtetls*. All the *shtetls*, one suspects, were rather different from the nostalgic personal and literary memories they provoked in the present generation. The Jews could not believe that they were going to be mass murdered. How could they? They lived, after all, before the Holocaust, whereas you and I live after it.

So it was only after the murder that the remnant rebelled. And after the magnificent rebellion, those who were left continued their struggle until liberation. They fought among Soviet partisans who were often understanding and friendly and sometimes hostile and murderous.

Cholawski was a teacher then and is still teacher, of mathematics and of Holocaust history, in Kibbutz Ein Hashofet. After the war, he became the head of the Soldiers', Fighters' and Pioneers' Survivors Association. This does not blur his analysis. On the contrary, it provides his historical analysis with the controlled emotion that makes it truly an important contribution to our vicarious experience of the central event in twentieth-century Jewish history, the central event of our time.

Yehuda Bauer
Kibbutz Shoval
Institute of Contemporary Jewry
Hebrew University, Jerusalem

Soldiers from the Ghetto

The city is lovely, quiet, and clean.

The view of the castle is breathtaking. It is built in the style of the Middle Ages. A bridge connects the castle to the marvelous, lake-filled park that completely encircles the castle. A long avenue lined with sturdy trees approaches the city from the castle. In the middle of the city is the town hall, opposite it a little square of shops and a great square of walled buildings around it. On the outskirts of the city are the churches with their greenery, the schools, the meadows and grasses, the high embankment, the synagogues, including the Kalte Shul, and Green Boulevard with its chestnut trees and lilacs. Quiet streets, well paved, lead to and from the center of town, which at night shimmers with pale lights. All this defines the beauty of the tiny city.

"Little Warsaw" . . .

Within these confines, a Jewish congregation lived for hundreds of years.

Deep in my heart I hold a childhood memory. On Green Boulevard, across from my window, at the street corner, there stood a lovely pine tree, tall and erect. It grew higher and higher. Its top reached the skies. It bestowed its beauty on the nearby trees with a touch of its leaves. One day the tree was struck by lightning and it collapsed.

This childhood memory has been with me as if it were part of my own shadow.

Part One

Nesvizh, Poland
1939

The war broke out on September 1. Receiving the call-up on the same day, I said good-bye to my father and my brothers and relatives and asked my brothers to take care of Father. As a parting gift, I received a small bag embroidered with a Star of David.

Within a few hours I reported to the Kletsk Military Camp. I thought I would be sent immediately to the front, but a day passed, two days, and I was still at the camp, along with others who also had been mobilized. There were rumors that the front had been broken through and that the Germans were advancing rapidly. When we asked why we were still waiting around, why we were not fighting, the answer was, "We have no arms." Was it possible that on the second day of the war, the Poles were without sufficient weapons to arm their troops?

What, then, was the meaning of the announcement made by the chief of staff on the eve of the war, "We won't yield a button"? If so, then the war was lost. The entire Polish line of defense did not have a leg to stand on. The radio began to broadcast continual frantic calls from the mayor of Warsaw urging the citizens to defend themselves.

13

After a week of suspense in the camp, I received a temporary discharge with instructions to remain on call in case of a renewed mobilization. I went back home to Nesvizh.

And all this time, the question remained, "Where was Poland's line of defense?"

On the morning of December 17, the town was swept by the rumor, "Die gedolim geyen" "The big ones are coming!" Planes appeared in the sky. Jews ran out from their houses staring at the planes, wondering if the aircraft were "ours" or "theirs." Henritsi, the Polish mayor, came galloping on his horse down Pilsudski Street, where I lived, warning everyone "The Bolsheviks are coming !" The Polish police ran about helter-skelter. We became frantic and hid.

Soon the rumblings of heavy artillery were heard. Tanks appeared on our street; the masses of steel shook the houses as they went past. Convoys of lorries filled with soldiers followed. The red stars on the tanks and on the caps of the soldiers declared that the Red Army was advancing to the front to fight the Germans.

At first, the streets were empty, but then, almost instantaneously, they were overrun with crowds. More curious than frightened, the people stood on the pavement viewing the Red Army in full mass. People began to applaud and throw flowers to the soldiers. Standing in the crowd were *ossadniks* ("colonists"), including demobilized officers who had come to settle the lands along the eastern frontier to create a Polish buffer zone. They had always regarded the Russians as "those damned Muscovites." But now they, too, threw flowers to the marching columns. Someone cheered: "They are going to help the Poles beat the bloody *Schwab.*"

For several hours tanks moved westward. A few remained in town. There was some firing of shots in the morning, and then silence.

We knew that a fundamental change had taken place, but we had no conception of what it was. Something within urged us to remain silent. In the afternoon, the radio broadcast the announcement by the Soviet minister of foreign affairs, Molotov, that the Polish government had abandoned the Polish people and fled. The Germans had retreated. The USSR ordered its armed forces to cross the frontier and take under its protection the Belorussian and Ukrainian people.

Public meetings were held in the market place. All the official orators made speeches on the same theme: "We have come to liberate you from the oppression of the Polish overlords, who drank your blood. From now on, every human being, regardless of race, sex, or religion, will be free."

At these meetings, representatives of the population were "elected" in accordance with the recommendations of the authorities. The candidates all sounded the same: "I don't know how to read or write. All I did was shepherd the nobleman's geese. My mother is a laundry woman, and my father works with a pick and shovel." This kind of speech appealed to the masses, and since these poor peasants were substantial evidence that the lowly could achieve the good life, support for the authorities grew.

Some, however, were skeptical. The local Jews had participated in the underground in the revolution of 1905. And there were those who remembered that the Bolsheviks, in 1917, stopped in the town on their way to Lodz and Warsaw and stirred the hearts and minds of the Jews with promises of the coming of the messiah. Redemption turned out to be beyond their grasp.

For many years afterwards, while they sat by the warm oven in the house of study between the afternoon and evening prayers or while they sipped hot tea in glasses during the long winter nights, Jews continued to tell stories of those days. The pain of these memories prompted the Jews to be wary of what was being said now. Above all, there hovered the question, "from what will we live?"

The feeling of deliverance soon vanished, and in its place crept instability and uncertainty. The principal question that gnawed at us was what this Soviet regime held in store for the Jews.

It was not long after that all the Jews had to open their shops in accordance with the orders of the "authorities." Officers, clerks, and officials who came from the east swooped down upon the stores. They did no bargaining, nor were they particular in what they chose. They bought everything within reach: boots, leather goods, cloth, socks, hats, watches. The smaller the item, the more valuable it seemed to them. They paid with brand new *czervontzes,* Soviet bills, fresh off the government presses. *Rubles* replaced *zlotys.*

The younger people knew less and hoped for more. They were relieved by their apparent redemption from the war. They were moved by the proclamations and slogans about justice and equality, by the homeliness of these Russians, and by the informality and charm of their folk songs:

My country, my broad land
Many are your woods and rivers and fields
I do not know
In the whole world
Such a land of freedom and liberty.

These songs captivated the hearts of the young. Films like *Petersburg Nights* and *Lenin in 1918,* with images of friendly, happy Russian peasants and of the zealous Lenin, were inspiring. I still have memories of these Russian films I saw in Vilna in my youth, in the days when it seemed that a film was more real than life itself. But with this newfound inspiration some of us sensed a gathering of brooding clouds shadowing the ideals of *Eretz Israel* and of everything Jewish in character and content.

The children sensed it too, especially those of the Tarbut "Culture" School for whom Hebrew was the natural daily language. They sensed it in the depth of their souls, for Judaism encompassed *Eretz,* the hope and the dream, and all that was beautiful in their lives. They were confused. For the first time, it seemed to them that the adults were powerless.

A Soviet way of life set in.

Sirotka, the commissar, wearing a Stalin cape, announced before a large public gathering, "Land for those without land; bread for those without bread; horses for those without horses."

But for some reason, these slogans, which initially stirred the masses, were now received coldly. The hearts were not inflamed. Food and merchandise had become scarce. The Jewish shops were emptied of their goods. The owners accumulated *czervontzes,* but could do nothing with them. Above some store fronts new signs appeared: *Narkompishtchepromtorg, Woyentorg, Gosbank, Promcombinat,* and others with what seemed like gibberish. The farmers, who had been accustomed to seeing the Jewish shops well stocked, yearned for days gone by. With the loss of their businesses, many of the Jews lost their means of livelihood. Their future became uncertain. Some of them had a reserve of money from the *knot* (or *knippl*), which was put aside for a daughter's wedding or for a needy day. But how long could one draw from such a source? After all, a *knot* was not a plant or an animal that grew. If not nourished, in one bite, two, it was gone.

The artisans, for the most part, continued to work in *artels.* Although it was a meager living, the artisans gave thanks for such a blessing. The *artels* were set up in the synagogues. The Kozimir Synagogue became a bicycle *artel*; the *Talmud Torah*, for carpenters; another for the cobblers.

The Kalte Shul was transformed by the authorities into a furniture warehouse, and the marketplace *shul* became a clubhouse with a young Jew as its director. Those who customarily prayed in the marketplace *shul* were bold enough

17

to approach the authorities and request that their place of worship remain a house of prayer. The answer was, "It is your own youth who demand it to be so."

In the streets, there were lines for bread, for soap, for sugar, for everything. People would come early just to find that others had arrived even earlier. This sort of competition led people to stand on line at midnight just to be at the front of the line of a shop opening the following morning.

Public activity was censored. People with questionable pasts and those with political records were summoned to *doprosses* ("interrogations"). Later, when I began to teach in the middle school, the secret police, the NKVD, invited me to one of their talks; my past was suspect. Presenting myself before them was a terrifying experience. I was seated before a tall, coarse peasant, a *hochol*, with slanted, evil eyes. He questioned me in a most "civilized" manner; the conversation made me anxious. The questions put before me concerned my business. I declared, "I am a worker." He jumped up in anger and great agitation. "What sort of worker? An artisan?" Although I could not recall my father ever having employed a worker or an apprentice, it seemed that this distinction, to my interrogator, was vital in deciding if I was a member of the proletariat, or something less *kosher*. I was released, under suspicion, shaken and angry.

Arrests began.

For selling a package of yeast on the black market, the penalty was one year imprisonment. When boards were burned in the tailor's *artel* by an iron carelessly set on the floor, someone was put in jail. Workers were arrested as British or American spys. Refugees arriving from western Poland without Soviet identity cards were transported to the inner regions of USSR or to the camps. Railway cars, dubbed *tieplushki* ("hothouses"), arrived at nearby Horodzei Station and, overnight, "suspected" persons were packed in and driven away never to be heard from again.

Then came the arrest of Yoel Rozovski, chairman of the Zionist organization, chairman of the *Tarbut* School, and a community leader, one who, for decades, had borne the heavy burdens of the Jewish community. He was respected and loved by all. He was arrested and sent away without a trace. A few days later, members of his family were taken into custody. His imprisonment and exile shocked the Jewish public. There was no doubt that this arrest was a direct blow against the very life core of the Jewish community.

Our street was lined with houses of wood and brick. Its roadway was paved with stone. Jews, Poles, and Belorussians lived there side by side. It was not the main street, but it was the longest one, leading to the railroad station fourteen kilometers away, and serving as an artery to the outside world. Most of the Jews on our street were artisans, farmers, and small tradesmen; a few were clerks, and lawyers.

I grew up on this street. At home was my father, Yitzhak, and my four brothers. My mother died young, and the burden of fatherhood and motherhood fell upon Father suddenly. All his life he was a worker. Fate tied my father, from morning till night, to his workshop in the cellar of our home and to the hammer, axe, and chisel with which he fashioned wood.

I remember the lathe at which he worked. It consisted entirely of one thin wooden slat in front and two on the sides with iron cones. At the top of the thin slat was a rope which would be pulled tight around a tree trunk, set to be turned. The "motor" operating the lathe was Father's foot stuck in the pedal, which was attached to the end of the rope. By pressing down and then releasing his foot, Father would cause the log to turn between the iron cones. Working for hours this way, raising and lowering the pedal with his foot,

Father would cut the wood. Tired, Father would come home at dusk to begin chiselling and shaping the wood he had spent all day cutting. My father maintained his family by strenuous toil.

Only the Sabbath could erase the greyness of the week. On Fridays, Mother would scrub the yellowed wooden floor. After cooking and washing, she would cover the table with a white tablecloth and set out the Sabbath candles. As she lit the Sabbath candles, tears would stream down her face, and the house would radiate light. Our hearts were kindled with warmth.

Returning from our prayers in *shul*, we would find the house filled with the scent of Sabbath delicacies. When we were all seated around the great square table near the elegant buffet carved by Father, there was a feeling of a divine presence among us. Father, with his ironed Sabbath shirt, groomed moustache and hair, would begin the *Kiddush*. Mother, beautiful, young, and shining with motherly tenderness and love, would then serve her delicious chicken dishes. Those days, indeed, were the loveliest and happiest days.

With Mother's death, the serenity and beauty vanished. Cares and worries filled our home. How to raise and support a family of five boys without a mother?

Sadness was pervasive. It seemed to soak into the walls, into the furniture, and into the very heart of our home. My brother Zalman left to study at the Hashomer Hechalutz Center in Vilna, Mordechai and Shabbtai to study abroad. With only my brother Moshe, my father, and I at home, the radio became a welcome companion. It helped lift the depression. I would stay up late at night with this magic box, listening to the sounds, especially the wonderfully sad gypsy music coming from Sofia. On Friday nights, father would return from *minyan* held at one of our neighbors' homes. The Sabbath candles would be burning, though now they reflected only gloom. Father would be dressed in his Sabbath attire, his face lean and distressed. We would hastily eat our Sabbath meal. Then we would close the shutters, and, in the outermost room, in the dark, Father, Uncle Shlomo, Moshe, and I would sit hovering over the radio, straining to catch the Hebrew broadcast from *Eretz Israel,* the week's *Haftorah* reading. Father and Uncle would hold the Bibles in their hands and, by the dim candlelight, would whisper the words. The radio voice was broken frequently by broadcast interference, and we would succeed in catching only bits of the reading. But for my father, these moments were joyous; they nourished his longing for the land of Israel. Tears would gather in his eyes, and he would recall the past, when ideals inspired actions.

As a young man, Father was a member of the *Poalei Zion* (Workers of Zion) movement, then still in the underground. It was a small group, attracting teachers and young workers. Avraham Mahtei was their leader and idol, a brilliant and talented orator who spread the teachings of the Zionist socialist movement. My father mentioned his name only with the deepest reverence. The circle met in the attic of Haizel Herzog, an elementary school teacher, and they listened to lectures given by guest speakers or local comrades. The group passed resolutions and established a school where Hebrew and Yiddish were taught. It was named after Ber Borochov. On holidays and on the Sabbath, they would go to *schodkes,* secret meetings of small groups, in the forest of Albe or in the woods around town. On certain evenings, they would gather in a closed room and hold literary meetings in honor of Mendele or Peretz. The curtains would be drawn, the shutters closed, and they would sing:

"Huliet, huliet baise vinten . . .
Ah, voss klogt ihr, kirchen golcken
Hert shoin oif, genug geshroken

21

Hobin eiere vilde tenner
Unser orim velt.

(Rage, oh rage on you bitter winds
Church bells, why do you ring?
Stop, you have frightened enough
With your wild tones
Our poor world.)

Father would tell us over and over again about the Jewish
self-defense during the 1905 pogroms. "Here," he would
point his finger and say with no small amount of drama, "in
the wall underneath the window was the safe for our
organization." I knew my father was responsible for this
cache, and he was proud to have made his contribution to the
organization. This was the most treasured of my father's
stories. Listening to the broadcasts from *Eretz* served to bring
back the pain of lost dreams for him. But from one Friday to
the next we would be nourished by these erratic meetings
with the Holy Land.

The small hopes rekindled by these Sabbath nights were
diminished by the wildly spreading flames that separated us
from the rest of the world. The first refugees arriving from
western Poland told stories of inexplicable humiliations and
sufferings inflicted by the Germans on the Jews. Polish
Jewry seemed on its way towards some fateful ordeal.

Directly in front of our house lived Rabbi Hirsch
Kalmanovitz. Reb Hirsch was a tall, lean Jew, quick in conversation and action. His wife, Sheine, was short and had a
quiet manner. She was slow in her movements and speech. As
different as they seemed outwardly, they complemented each
other.

Early each morning, we could see Reb Hirsch opening the
shutters in his usual brisk way, sweeping the path in front of
his house, and then rushing off with his prayer shawl to wor-

ship in the first *minyan*. Sheine would rise later, prepare a light breakfast, and leisurely open their groceries, taking her customary seat by the doorway. Prayers over, Reb Hirsch would return home, grab a light snack, and then retire to the sanctity of his little room, the nerve center of the entire family. There he would go over the ledgers, the accounts, and the bills. Reb Hirsch had three daughters and two sons, and he took great care in supporting them, both financially and spiritually. Characteristically, he married off a son and the older daughters to children of neighboring families so that he could keep a close eye on their affairs. I recall a meeting between Reb Hirsch and my uncle Reb Aaron Levine shortly before the outbreak of the war. My uncle was complaining that he never saw his children, now that they were married and had moved away. Reb Hirsch chided Reb Levine. "See what you have done to yourself? You have scattered your children all over the globe, two sons in Australia, an only daughter in Belgium. Now, in your old age, you are wretched and alone. A Jew should marry off his children close to his home; he should care for Jewish survival close to his home; he should do everything close to his home. The home is the source of strength."

Reb Hirsch owned two grocery stores, one located in his home, the other in the marketplace. The state of both his business and his family was as vital to him as his religion and his learning. Once the daily affairs were put in order, Reb Hirsch would sit down with his books. An avid reader, he would pick up a book on Karl Marx or classical literature as easily as the *Talmud*. He wrote articles on practical Zionism and on his messianic beliefs.

In the spring and summer, it was his custom to take solitary walks in the evening in the green fields beyond the town. He would enjoy the brightness of the world and reflect. Meeting someone on the way, young or old, he would be the first to acknowledge him with a bow and a greeting. Between the afternoon and evening prayers, he would sit alone in his corner of the syngogue and, by candlelight, study the *Gemorrah*.

Reb Hirsch was very sharp. Although his hearing was impaired and had worsened with the years, he spoke rapidly, gesturing and fluttering his hands. His deafness forced his quick perception. Ever since my childhood, I could remember being amazed by and attracted to his keenness of mind and his wisdom. Since then I have never known any other person as perceptive and astute as he.

I frequently visited Reb Hirsch, especially during the long winter evenings when my father would be resting after a long day's work. Reb Hirsch would always greet me cordially, looking forward to an evening of discussion and philosophy. When I left for Vilna to further my studies, Reb Hirsch continued to show interest in my activities. I would always call upon him when I returned home on the holidays, anxious to continue our discussions, and I always left his home filled with new answers and renewed faith.

Late in December of 1939, I returned to Vilna, my spiritual homeland, where I had spent my youth and studied, where I went hungry, and where I had been happy and in love. Vilna was the window to the outside world where I could gather the news of the activities of Jews beyond the boundaries of Poland. I wanted to find out if it was possible to make *aliyah,* immigration to *Eretz.* The winter that year was severe. I reached Lida, and with the help of the members of the movement, and wrapped tightly and warmly against the snow and ice and chilling winds, I travelled on to Vilna, about one hundred kilometers away, in a sleigh.

Entering Vilna, I walked through familiar streets: Stefanska, Zavalna, Troki, Rudnitzka, Breite, and Ozheshkova. I walked about breathless, like a prisoner released from his cell. But something was wrong. The streets seemed alien; the atmosphere was tense and the people nervous. I went to visit the *Tarbut* Teachers' Seminary where I had studied for five years. The place was deserted and unkept.

On Novogrudska Street, I met a companion of mine from school days and from the movement. She told me that her husband had advanced in rank with the authorities and was now a "labor leader." At Venglova, I met with some of the members of the *Hanhaga Roshit* (Executive of the Youth Movement), and with Abba Kovner, my friend from the days in the *Vilna Ken Hashomer Hatzair* Youth Center. They told me of the hundreds of members of the movement concentrated in Vilna, anxious to make *aliyah*. But the list was long and the chances for success slight.

I listened to stories about *Eretz,* and I read with great interest a booklet called *Al Mashuot Polin* ("By Polish Ruins"), which expressed the sense of despair I felt in my heart.

I left Vilna for home soon after, my head reeling with what I had seen and learned.

In Lida I boarded a train to Baranovichi and entered a small compartment. The people inside sat bundled in their winter clothes. I made my way through the crowd of people, coats, and scarves toward a vacant corner. Pulling my coat tightly around me, I sat by a window covered with frost. A raw wind came through the cracks.

Coming down the aisle, to my surprise, I saw a young woman I had known before, Yehudit Michalovska. She was dressed in a uniform, a military coat and a leather belt. She had the appearance of a typical Komsomol.

She spotted me and, with a slight look of welcome, sat down beside me. She whispered in Yiddish, "How are you?" "Well" was all I said. Indeed, it was Yehudit. Despite the severity of the uniform, the tenderness of her lovely young face shone through. During the early 1930s, as a young girl in Vilna, she had studied at the Hebrew Gymnasium and had

25

been a member of the *Betar* Revisionist Youth Movement. Her classmates, who were under my leadership in the *Bama'aleh* group, had introduced her to the *Ken Hashomer*. She was quite young, smart, and capable, and we spent many hours together talking about the *k'vutzah* ("group"). She was well liked for her manners, her charm, and her intellect. She was happy, it seemed.

Some time later, I heard a rumor that Yehudit had become active in student Communist circles. I was sorry and disappointed to hear of her change. I had had such hopes for her.

To see her now, it was obvious that she was fulfilling some party mission. She seemed fanatical in her faith. I suddenly felt afraid; she could not have forgotten my own loyalties. It was possible, too, that she could guess what I was doing on this train from Lida, a railroad junction to Vilna. Perhaps she thought of turning me in to the authorities as a conspirator and agitator.

She did nothing, however—just sat with me for the entire trip. Except for what our brief intermittent glances revealed, nothing was said. I could not help but envision her back in the Gymnasium, at the Vilna *Ken,* laughing, speaking Hebrew, making plans for Israel. How could all of this have been cast aside? Would there remain some latent longings hidden inside her that would one day surface and carry her back to the dreams and ideals she once nurtured and embraced? At my train stop, we parted, again with only a slight nod. I watched the train pull out, as she remained immobile in her seat. I never saw her again. I learned that she was among the first to be shot in the Lida ghetto by the Nazis.

I had accepted a teaching position at the *Tarbut* School in the summer preceding the war. With the start of the school year, however, an official ruling allowed only the teaching of Yiddish. Hebrew was prohibited. Without the language of our culture, teaching was frustrating. Most depressing of all were the children who gazed at us with large, moist eyes, questioning why they were being deprived of their hope, their Hebrew language. Just a few months before, Hebrew rolled off their tongues in laughter, in play; the streets hummed with sounds of life and joy. Now, suddenly, to speak Hebrew was forbidden and gravely punishable.

With the keen perception of the innocent, the children understood this outrage and only overtly lived within the law. Secretly, however, they devised ways to avoid the ruling and its consequences. A child would pass by and whisper, "I hid *Lashon Vasefer* in my house." "Yesterday we lit the Chanukah candles at home and I sang *Yeshuati*." The children would anxiously trade indiscretions among themselves. One day a twelve-year-old student of mine, Estherke Harlap, approached me. She had a sister in *Eretz* who had gone there before the war with youth aliyah and was in Ben Shemen. Estherke looked at me tenderly and said, "I dreamt of Channele last night." These dreams inspired the children and renewed their hopes.

Restrictions lead to suspicion and fear among friends. My companion at work, Shaul Friedstein, was a member of the movement in the past, a graduate of the *Tarbut* Teachers Seminary in Vilna, and the former principal of the local Hebrew school. Many an evening the two of us spent in secret, speaking frankly to each other of our disillusionment and despair. We were both amazed with the system of teaching, particularly of giving marks. The most used word in the teachers' lounge was "achievement," the only measure of success. Achievement was gauged by the number of good marks compared with the number of failures. Since the formula of socialist competition had also penetrated into the school system, the teacher's achievement was measured by the percentage of his student's performance. So it followed that a teacher who generously distributed passing marks at-

27

tained a higher rate of achievement, thus coming out ahead in the socialist competition. A teacher who demanded more of his pupils and who examined each grade carefully, attained a distinctly lower evaluation in achievement and, consequently, failed in the competition. These teachers were then criticized by the inspectors and encouraged to follow the example of their comrades—to distribute more passing marks to improve their own level.

Teaching Yiddish was soon forbidden and by order of the government, only Russian was allowed. I was assigned to teach mathematics and nature to the lower grades, in Russian.

One evening, we were called to a general teachers' meeting—Poles, Belorussians, and Jews. On the agenda was the election of the Nesvizh Teachers' Committee. Presiding were several Russians, all party members. Among the candidates was Shaul Friedstein, my co-worker. One of the female teachers in the Yiddish school, Zaltzman, who had been a member of the Bund in the past, rose from her seat and suggested that Shaul's name be removed from the list of candidates because of his Zionist affiliation. Zionism, she declared, was a reactionary movement not to be tolerated. She spoke with intense passion, and when she concluded, there was a great silence and an electrified tension in the hall.

I asked permission to speak. "If you mean to invalidate Shaul Friedstein on the basis of his Zionist background, you must, consequently, declare most of the Jews here unfit, for they, too, are Zionists. Hebrew is our living language, and the allegiance we have for Israel is sincere and unyielding. We will not be persuaded otherwise, nor will we tolerate pressure from anyone to think differently. History will prove us right."

A thunder of applause swept through the hall. It was an ex-

28

pression of support and defiance. Shaul was elected by a decisive majority. I felt a great victory though I was convinced that I would have to pay dearly for the words I had uttered in public. All through the night I was on the alert for a knock at the door. None came. Perhaps *they* hadn't understood exactly what I had said since I had spoken in Polish. Or perhaps there were other considerations weighing more heavily than my indiscretion. Nevertheless, it appeared that I was not going to pay for speaking out against the government.

The members of *Hashomer Hatzair* tried their best to stick together with the coming of the Russians. Some of the older members, those who had been at the *Hechalutz* Training Center, left for Vilna, to the *Hashomer Hechalutz* Center. But among those members who remained, personal bonds deepened. I became very close with Lolek Abilevitz, Yankele Harlap, and Shalom Volokayanski.

Lolek and Yankele returned home from the war and from a German prison camp in December of 1939. Shalom returned from the front. Like the others who straggled home, the feeling of delight at being spared quickly vanished. As if they were strangers, they felt a difference in everything once familiar—the way of life, the people, their spirit. Some were able to accept this, change, and integrate easily into the changed society. There were those who publicly renounced former ties. But there were those who remained faithful to their feelings for *Eretz*.

Lolek, Yankele, and Shalom were loyal members of the movement. Lolek and Yankele were the best of friends. Lolek was a handsome fellow, of medium height, broad and solid. When he was a child he lost his father, but his mother had been generous with her love, instilling *Yiddishkeit* within him. He was optimistic, intelligent, and realistic. It was difficult to imagine Lolek in a state of despair. His hearty laugh was a delight to us all. After finishing his studies at the *Tarbut* School, he went on to study in a Polish Gymnasium. He joined the movement and was quickly delegated much responsibility. Before his mobilization, Lolek succeeded in finding a way into the hearts of some of the best youth in town, bringing them into the fold of the movement. During the war, he was captured by the Germans and held prisoner until his release in December. Yankele was quiet, always serious, but, like Lolek, he was a good worker, a strong fellow, decisive, and always willing to volunteer. He remained inconspicuous, but rose to great heights during times of crisis.

Shalom had studied for years in the neighboring towns and had been active as a leader in the movement. Lolek, Yankele, and Shalom were drafted into the army together and served in the same brigade, the Twentieth Division. In the summer of 1939, their unit was stationed in the vicinity of Modlin. The three of them, in uniform, would visit the nearby summer camps of the movement, as well as the branches of the movement in the adjacent towns, speaking to the youth and educating them to the movement's policies and ideals. Once they returned to Nesvizh, the three were just as active in the movement as ever.

One day we received a note, smuggled from Vilna: "Come immediately to Lida. The password at the station is *A geruss fun feter Zhame* ("Regards from Uncle Zhame.") We recognized the handwriting as that of one of the leaders of the *Hashomer Hatzair*.

Perhaps this was the chance we had been waiting for. Lida, with its concentration of *chalutz* youth, was the vital connection to Vilna and then to *Eretz*. Lida was hope!

Lolek, Yankele, and Shalom were chosen to go. When they arrived in Lida, they were told they were not to be transfered to Vilna and then to Israel, but, instead, they were to be connections in smuggling *chalutz* youth from transfer points close to the border to Vilna. Lolek, at first, was angry and demanded transport to Vilna. Yankele accepted his orders unquestioningly. "It's a miracle we have such a place as Nesvizh," Yankele said. "Otherwise, where else could three fellows like us be roped in all at one time?" Suddenly Lolek realized the honor bestowed on them in this great responsibility. They became eager to start.

The organization was a simple one. Shalom remained in Lida. His task was to organize the men going on foot and to send them on to Yankele and Lolek, who took positions in two villages, Divinishki and Sokoli, along the border.

Circumstances at the border did not remain static, and plans to smuggle people across changed frequently. At first, the border was practically wide open, and clever ones were able to steal across. Those quick to get a lift to Vilna with the drivers of military vehicles were pitied as poor refugees who wanted to get back home to Vilna. Soon, the soldiers uncovered this ruse and began sending them back. A new tactic was undertaken. When one was caught, he would say, "I want to go to Russia. I don't want to continue living in capitalistic Lithuania." The soldiers would then "return" him to Lithuania, it was disloyal to leave. After all, crossing a border was not a child's game.

There were other tricks, but gradually every method became inadequate. More and more people were detained. Winter added to the hardships. There was freezing cold and snow. The humorists maintained that Siberia had moved closer since the border had been erased. Those who tramped through the snow to reach the border would sink deep into the drifts until they were ready to drop. One of our comrades hid in a stable after he had succeeded in crossing. His legs froze, and when he came to Vilna, they had to amputate all his toes to save his life.

Yankele, Lolek, and Zilla Gillerovitz, another of our members, made more and more visits to Lida to keep in touch with the connections. The constant shortage of funds made the work hard, but this never stopped the group. Clothes and watches were sold for quick cash. No price was too dear. Then came another source of trouble. Groups could not get across the border without being seen by the peasants, who began to blackmail them.

"The pressures and risks are tremendous," reported Shalom. "We are responsible for the safety of these youths. We need to be quick, to exploit every possibility and opportunity, no matter how slight the chance, no matter how risky.

"There was a group of young men from the branch of the movement in Wohlin and with them, a young girl from the intermediate age group, the *zofim*. I refused to include her in the escape plan. First of all, we were sending only adults. Second, we had to be strict about physical fitness and capabilities. The cold and snow demanded great perserverance. Despite my reasoning, the young men were adamant in her joining the group. They declared that she would not disappoint us and that they were even prepared to carry her in their arms just to get her across. I still wasn't convinced. Then the girl spoke. She insisted that she would go, come what may. She spoke with such passion and conviction that we were dwarfed by her emotions. That same evening she made the crossing without a mishap."

The border gradually grew tighter and finally closed shut. Not even a bird could get through.

Soon after, an emissary arrived from Vilna. It seemed that he had a "reliable man" who was willing to take one at a time across the border. Yankele was the first to go. He went with our many good wishes and hopes. He never made it. We did not know what went wrong. Days passed and we heard nothing. Shalom, frustrated and angered, decided to escape on his own and try his luck in the south at the Hungarian or Rumanian border. Zilla and Lolek returned to Nesvizh. There would be no more border crossings.

Those of us in the movement met more frequently. Contacts with the younger groups were tightened. There still smoldered some hope that good tidings would come from Vilna and that the border would be opened. We waited. Some time later we received a letter from the town of Verkuta. It was from Yankele. He wrote, "If the day comes and one of you is privileged to come to the shores of that warm land, remember me, your brother, perishing on the frozen shores of Siberia."

Meanwhile, in Nesvizh, connections between the groups of younger members of the movement had to be maintained and operations planned. Among those who assumed leadership were Zilla Gillerovitz and Hedva Lahovitzka. There were no educational materials available. The meetings, therefore, were based on what we remembered. We encouraged friendship, devotion, and faith. Halkin's book, *Bar Kochba,* the only book available, supplied material for group discussions.

Hedva went to Slonim to meet with Yitzhak Zalmanson and over thirty representatives from neighboring towns. It was a moving experience and productive as well. This conference testified to the existence of an underground movement, and gave us renewed strength and encouragement.

After much deliberation, we decided that it was of vital importance to preserve whatever remained of our heritage. When the Russians first came, everyone was happy. In the beginning, the Soviets were generous, handing out cigarettes and money. Many at home had drifted with the tide and renounced their faith. We decided that the time had now come to work against the current. The first plan of action was to save the *Tarbut* School Library. It had been our greatest asset, our source of education. Now, the *Tarbut* School stood isolated and desolate. Whoever passed would be overcome by waves of warm memories. A group of us—Aryeh Shapiro,

Monki Bonkovski, Motke Fruman, Notte and Yizthak Harlap, Laibel Slutzki, Yitzhak Perlman, and Shabbtai, my brother, among others—were in charge of this operation. We chose the *shtiebel* in the Kalte Shul to house the books from the *Tarbut* School. To get the younger members involved, we gave them the major responsibility for this operation. They climbed through the windows and removed the books from the shelves. They filled their specially lined coats with as many books as they could and still be able to walk without creating suspicion. Others transferred the books in baskets covered with food, under the very noses of patrols and detectives.

The group prepared a clandestine catalog so any book could be located within a matter of seconds. They were proud of their operation. They continued to have regular meetings. The younger members, under the leadership of Zilla, organized themselves into several groups to conduct individual meetings. At first they held their meetings while on hikes; later the *shtiebel* became the central meeting place. Under the guise of an informal gathering, they would bring cigarettes and frozen apples. They prepared their own version of an oath and lit candles. They decided to put out a newspaper to express their feelings, dreams, and loneliness. Since Aryeh Shapiro had been the editor of the school newspaper, *Hayainu,* he was put in charge. The youngsters began to write articles and other short pieces in a thick notebook. Every fortnight and on holidays the paper came out. The reading of the paper became the main event at get-togethers and meetings.

The group also established a common fund. The books that were available—those of Bialik, Tschernichovsky and Ahad Ha'am—were passed from hand to hand. Zilla brought them information about the continued existence of the movement. They began to feel that they belonged to something large and important. They received the paper

'Mi-Ma'amakim' "Out of the Depths," and other clandestine publications. They collected money for *Keren Kayemet* to be forwarded to Vilna and then on to *Eretz*. Soon they too eagerly awaited their turn to escape to *Eretz*.

Since the fall of 1939, hundreds of refugees had arrived from western Poland. They came first in small groups, but gradually with the advance of time and fear, families flocked to the security of our town and others close to Russia. Some travelled further into Russia itself before the border became impassable. All told of the Germans and their "new order." Those who settled among us assimilated easily with the local Jews despite differences in dialect and manners. Among the refugees were educated people, brimming with knowledge, wisdom, and poetry.

Schlomo Dikman of Warsaw resided with the Eisenbuds after his relocation. Dikman had a talent for languages. He was extremely erudite, particularly in literature and poetry. He had translated Bialik into Polish, and a few days before the war, his translations had appeared in Warsaw. Dikman succeeded in forwarding a single copy of his book to Vilna so that it might get to *Eretz Israel* and be preserved.*

One autumn day as I was reading in the Radzivil gardens, a man approached me. He was of medium height, middle aged, and graying at the temples, but he had a look of youth and vitality. Glancing at the book in my hand, he spotted the strange square lettering. He asked, "Is that a Yiddish book?" I replied yes. We began to talk. His name was Shmuel Zaromb.

* Dikman was exiled to Siberia for his "subversive" activities. Only after many years in Russian concentration camps did he finaly reach Israel. There, to great acclaim, he translated the Greek and Roman classics into Hebrew. Dikman died in 1965.

35

He was staying at the home of Reb Itsche, the book binder, in one of the tumbledown alleyways of the Mikhalishok. There he had a narrow, cold room with a bed, a table, and a single chair. I was impressed with the man, with his honesty, his loyalty, and his stoicism. We met often. Every talk with him took me on a journey through Jewish and world literature. He spoke bitterly against those who had renounced their own heritage. He mourned the cultural wilderness in which the Russian Jews lived. He spoke of his Hebrew poetry translated into Yiddish and published by the *Hechalutz* Center. His sincere words and deep emotions revealed his abiding love and ties with the members of *Hechalutz*.

One evening during Chanukah, sitting in my room with a glass of tea and a plate of *latkes,* I told him of the attempts to break a trail through to *Eretz* via the mountains of the Caucasus. His eyes filled with tears of hope: "Oh, would that I were able to leave now for those mountains of redemption."

During one of my visits to his humble room in Mikhalishok, Shmuel read his sonnets to me. I remember but one line; the memory of his reading stirs me to this day: "Es klingt in mir das lied fun nahrois Bovel" ("Within me vibrates the song of the rivers of Babylon"). He sent his works to a Jewish writer in Moscow, but they were never printed. In the near future, he would take those sonnets with him to his untimely end.

Our Jewish heritage was being crushed and destroyed, in business, in school, at home, and within each heart.

I looked forward to the smuggled letters and articles that came to me from Vilna. They contained bits of news of *Eretz* and the movement. I read these articles in the middle of the night, in secret, well aware that if I were caught with these writings, I would be condemned to years of imprisonment and exile. These, however, did little to relieve the dark, brooding despair that seemed to all but consume my hopeful spirit.

One harsh, wintry night, I knocked on Rabbi Hirsch's door. I felt a need to talk with him. The house was dark except for a faint light flickering within the Rabbi's little room. Reb Hirsch greeted me at the door, and graciously led me to his study. He sat before me, at first absorbed in his thoughts. Gradually he began to speak.

"What will be, *Shalom,* what will be? Why, it's the beginning of the end. This cold will soon freeze us all. How long can a living being survive in a frost? Not a ray of light, not a ray of light!"

At first he lowered his voice as if apprehensive that what he was saying would be heard outside, but then his voice began to grow in power and strength. Although his speech was erratic, his thoughts were absolutely clear and lucid, an intellectual thread binding them together.

"See what they have done to us. The *Kehillah* is no more, the *Talmud Torah* is gone. Synagogues, we have none; no schools, no holidays, no *chalutzim,* no *Eretz Israel,* nothing, nothing. We are going towards nothing at all."

His hands began to flutter wildly, their shadows filling the little room. "Every living body needs a bit of warmth. Even when the source of heat is distant, it can warm a bit. But they have stopped the flow of heat.

"Our Nesvizh is not a large town, but it lies on the road between Minsk and Vilna. From here people would go off to study. Here came the great rabbis of Mir, Wolozhin, and Slobodka. For generations the greatest rabbis lived among us, since the Jewish community began in the fifteenth century. According to legend, Shaul Wohl, the Jewish King of Poland, lived here. The Radzivils built one of their beautiful palaces here, and brought in the latest innovations of the West. Two hundred years ago they set up a printing press with a Jew in charge.

"Here, too, the great Rabbi Shlomo Maimon was born.

37

Rabbi Moishe Neshvezher ascended from here to *Eretz* in the year 1800, together with the pupils of the great Gaon of Vilna. E.M. Dick lived here. Rappaport wrote his famous novels here. Zionists lived here and communicated with Herzl. Correspondents wrote to *Ha-Z'firah.* Your own Rabbi Zvi Ha-Cohen Moshvitski was a steady correspondent of this paper, which was distributed throughout Russia and beyond.''

I sat bound to my chair, listening to all the Reb Hirsch was saying and watching the intensity of his motion and emotion. Events, personalities, bits of tales: with these, Reb Hirsch painted a great canvas of life in this town, stretching across generations of Jews, but now fraying.

But I couldn't help thinking, even with all this sadness, that with every ordeal, came a birth of new spiritual currents in Judaism. So it was with the *Hassidim,* with the *Haskala,* with Zionism, all arising despite riots, slaughters, *pogroms.* Could it be this way again, now? It had to be that all this would spark new Jewish response. It could not be otherwise.

Though flesh burned, need the spirit be consumed?

Reb Hirsch continued speaking excitedly, and he seemed, in my eyes, to be greater than I had ever seen him before. The dim light of the kerosene lamp lit up his long pale face, the small, curly, ashen beard, the gleam in his eye. He was a prophet from the past.

Late that evening, I returned home with a heavy heart.

June 26, 1941

On the street corner opposite my house stood a signpost. Scrawled on it was one word in Russian "Eastwards." The Russian soldiers were retreating. They dragged their feet through the town, the sound of their boots filling the streets. With their arms at their sides and faces to the ground, the Russians walked by, powerless and defeated. On seeing the signpost, some shook their heads in disbelief and anger. As they continued on their way up the street and out of town, a stillness descended on Nesvizh.

Since the struggle between the Germans and the Russians, the front had shifted hundreds of kilometers eastward. Where was the stronghold? Where was the defense force? One of the Red Army officers, with a look of beaten pride, said, "Don't worry. In another two or three weeks, we'll be back." We wanted to believe this, but we wondered what would happen in these next few weeks until they returned.

Shortly after the war broke out, a wave of good tidings swept through the city. Zarhin, the young musician, strutted down Wlienska Street, joking with those he met on the way: "Now, who wants to ride to Warsaw?" He had received news that Warsaw was already "ours." But now the Soviet soldiers were ordered to retreat eastwards.

Panic set in immediately. By the end of the day after the retreat, the city was practically devoid of Jews. Only the old people remained. Here and there a son or daughter stayed behind, refusing to leave parents or younger brothers and sisters. Some stayed, finding it too difficult to part with possessions.

I said goodbye to my father and younger brother, Moshe, whom my father would not allow to leave. I went eastwards in the direction of the "New City," together with Lolek Abilevitz, Hedva Lahovitzka, Siomka Farfel, and Mira Epstein, a member of the *Hanhaga Roshit,* who had been visiting relatives in our city. We gave the city one final look; we were among the last to leave. The streets were deserted and quiet. Everything seemed dead. At the outskirts of the city we came upon a family in a wagon pulled languidly by an old mare. We hitched a ride. Where we would end up, we did not know. We did not even know where the Germans were, though we could guess they had already parachuted several hundred kilometers beyond us. Traveling in the wagon, I was aware of

39

the fateful difference between the thunderous onslaught of the Germans and the feeble pace of our escape.

Near what had been the Polish-Russian border, not far from our town, hundreds of Jews were running helter-skelter. Russian cavalry soldiers caught up with us and ordered us back to the city. We were all told to report to the *voyencomat,* the mobilization office. The mass of Jews, on foot, in wagons, in groups and alone, made their way back to Nesvizh. The mobilization office was deserted, so there was nothing left for us but to return to our homes, bolt the doors, and lock the windows. We sat in our houses, waiting for the unexpected.

Suddenly, like a raging fire on a hot day, word spread that there was bread in the bakery. Momentarily disregarding their frightful expectations, people came pouring out of their houses. It was as if a frenzy of hunger had taken hold. They broke into the Berezin and Lipshitz bakeries and began snatching up loaves of bread from the shelves and sacks of flour from the storeroom. Crowds of people broke through the doors, running out the back with their booty. Somehow they knew that this would be their last opportunity to get food.

Shalom Cholawski   *Zalman (Ziama) Cholawski*

Lolek Abilevitz   *Yaacov (Yankele) Harlap*

41

Shalom Zur (Volochviansky)   *Zilla Gillerovitz*

Freidl Lachovitzka (Eichenwald)   *Siomka Farfel*

Nathan Messer

Moshe Damessek

Shmuel Nissenbaum

Hirsh Possessorski

Binyamin Vilitovsky   *Monik Yosselevski (Yaron)*

The Author, Shalom Cholawski

Addressing a protest rally in Germany against the deportation of the "illegal" Exodus immigrants, 1947.

Part Two

Throughout the night, the perimeter of the city was bombarded. The Germans entered with the dawn.

A German officer broke into our house, waving a pistol and searching wildly for Russian soldiers.

At the street corner, a German soldier replaced the sign "Eastwards" with one reading *Nach Moskau*. Groups of Russian prisoners of war were brought into the synagogue courtyard. They lay hungry and exhausted. The Germans moved among them, kicking them with their heavy shoes.

One of the soldiers began beating a prisoner. He raised the man to his feet and cursed him with every punch. The prisoner, a short fellow with dull Mongolian features, did not know why the German had singled him out or what he was raving about. He stood there, not resisting the blows. Suddenly, he lifted his hand and, with a terrific sweep, slapped his attacker powerfully and squarely on the cheek. Blood trickled slowly down the German's face. For a moment they stared at each other. One man seething with anger, the other calm. Several Germans brusquely shoved the man to a place behind the fence. A volley of shots echoed in the air.

I witnessed the scene from my window.

Within a few days, the Germans set the town "in order." One could hear the rumble of bombing in the distance. The Jews stayed locked in their houses. We were still waiting and hoping; maybe the others would return.

Toward evening, in the closed courtyards of the houses, Jews gathered secretly to hear and pass on the latest encouraging news. Although there was no truth to whatever information we heard, it sustained us and gave us hope. There was a Jew, the son-in-law of Mayevski, the *shoychet,* who carried out the ritual slaughter of animals for market. He was a short, thin man with a sparse beard, and he demonstrated a most prolific imagination. He turned out to be our primary source for news that he said he obtained from a "top source, whose identity could not be revealed." During the first days after the coming of the Germans, the *shoychet* disclosed news of crushing blows against the enemy. He supplied exact places and numbers: not far from Gomel, five German planes shot down; near Ursha, many German tanks smashed. This went on day after day, with new, startling events related in detail. Nobody would deny these news items, for in our hearts, this was what we longed to hear. Even though there might have been doubts, no one ventured to voice them. The mere sound of good news brought relief.

With the passing of the days, we were able to identify the planes flying eastward. They were all German, leaving little doubt as to how the war was progressing. Even the new accounts from the *shoychet* became less and less optimistic. The echoes of the shelling gradually died away. The Jews were soon bombarded with new ordinances: "*Verboten* to walk on the pavement; *verboten* to go out beyond the city limits; *verboten* to go into a Christian home; *verboten* to carry on a conversation with a Christian in the street; *verboten* to buy necessities from farmers; *verboten* . . ." Then came the order for all Jews to wear a white ribbon, ten centimeters wide, and a yellow badge. The regulations increased in number and severity.

With these unreasonable demands, our main concern was no longer the orders, the lack of food, or the ending of the war. We finally realized that it was a question of survival itself. Orthodox Jews, however, held steadfastly to the belief that we would be saved. We were protected by the blessing of Reb Meirke, one of the greatest rabbis and geonim of the town. His blessing was, "You will not be pampered by too much good; nor will you suffer excessive troubles." The first half came true as predicted, so it must be that the second will also come to pass.

On June 30, the members of the former Jewish *kehillah* were assembled, and a *Judenrat* was established under the German-appointed chairmanship of Maghalief. He was a Warsaw refugee, an attorney. Nobody in town knew him, and the fact that he was not a local person aroused distrust. As chairman of the *Judenrat,* he alone accounted for us to the German command.

Two weeks after the coming of the Germans, my brothers came home. Mordechai had been studying in Lida, and Zhame with the *Hashomer Hatzair* group in Vilna. With the bombing of Vilna, Zhame left the city by train, going east. The train was bombed near Lida. The homecoming of my brothers was a joyous occasion despite our anxiety. Zhame had much to tell me about the Vilna group. A few days later Zerah Zilberberg and Gedalya Shayek came to stay with us on their way to Bialystok. From them I heard additional information about the Vilna group. They were active members. Gedalyahu had a tempestuous personality. I remember the day after they arrived, Gedalya stepped out onto the street and chanced upon a *shegetz* ("young gentile") who taunted him with insults. Gedalya, without a moment's hesitation or regard to consequences, struck him. Gedalya and Zerah were destined to be vital participants in the revolt of the Bialystok ghetto.

The tension increased. On September 1, all Jews were ordered to leave their living quarters along the main streets and move to the side streets, particularly near the alleys. We moved to the back part of our house; its windows faced a side street.

Along with all our other fears, we were concerned that the youngsters would not be receiving their Jewish education. We knew that we were the only ones who could provide this so we

51

gathered at my home—Lolek Abilevitz, Siomka Farfel, Hedva Lahoritzka, Zilla Gillerovitz, and myself. We decided to organize those between the ages of eleven and twelve into youth groups with the purpose of bringing them together and giving them companionship and courage in these times of confusion and despair. Youngsters age sixteen and seventeen who belonged to the underground groups of the movement during the Soviet regime united into one strong force. Among them, Slibovski, who had studied at the Vilna Seminary, provided capable leadership. We could do nothing for those under the age of eleven, but we were hopeful that the older Jewish youth would now be strong in numbers and faith.

I wrote out a program of activities for youths of different ages. Several faded pages have survived, and I can decipher several lines: "Work program for groups with the coming of the Germans," "Judaism—its Essence and Revelation," and "The Third *Aliyah* and its Formation."

On October 18, all Jewish males age fifteen and over were assembled in the marketplace. The Germans took two hundred hostages and imposed a ransom: all the town's leather goods and clothing in exchange for our lives. The townspeople brought all that was demanded. The Germans wanted the Jews to get accustomed to this kind of assemblage and discipline. The next day the Germans, once again, asked for a ransom, this time for a half million rubles and two and a half kilograms of gold. The Jews somehow collected the money and the gold, with the help of some of the non-Jews who, as moral people, felt the injustice. Tomako, a teacher in the Polish Gymnasium, contributed his share as a show of defiance against the Germans.

On October 20, my uncle, Reb Aaron Levine, set out on foot with another Jew for Horodzei to perform a circumcision. Both of them were captured by the Germans before they reached their destination. Reb Levine and his companion, the grandfather of the infant, were brought to Glinishtze and killed.

That day I had been harvesting potatoes at Alba, near Glinishtze. It was afternoon and there was a stillness in the air. Suddenly I heard several shots. I knew it prefigured something ill. When I returned home that evening, I found out who the targets of those shots were. The murders angered and agitated the Jews of the town. How could they shoot upstanding, pious old men? The murders forced us to discard any false conceptions we might have been harboring. Thoughts about terrible things that might be coming began to cross our minds, but our imaginations proved limited.

On October 22, Morris Leder, Gershon Pik, and Israel Lampert were caught buying potatoes from a farmer, and were shot. Dr. Ginsberg was arrested for allowing wounded Russian POWs to sing Russian songs during his shift at the hospital.

I was transferred from drying fruits and vegetables in the factory, to digging peat. I worked with Lolek, Shaul Friedman, Noah Tcharni, and others. We worked in the fields, far away from the city.

With every echo of cannon fire reverberating in the distance, we hoped that we were hearing the advance of the Russians fighting back. But when we returned to town at dusk, instead of greeting our saviors, we would be confronted with bitter ordinances and horrible stories of the events of the day.

At 8:00 A.M., October 30, 1941, the entire Jewish population of Nesvizh was ordered to gather in the square to have their papers examined. We were full of dread. We imagined all sorts of reasons for the order. Maybe the Germans only intended to ransack our homes and then we would be able to return to them. Perhaps they would take some of us as hostages, again for ransom. No one mentioned that third thought; it was too shocking. Word had come from refugees from western Poland of an execution of twenty to thirty young Jewish men on the pretext that they were Communists. No, that would never happen here. We decided that we were allowing our worse fears to overshadow our clear judgment. The Germans just wanted to examine our papers. Reb Meirke's blessing would turn out to be fateful.

We did not know that just the day before, the Polish and Belorussian population had been summoned urgently to dig pits on the estate of Prince Radzivil and along the road to Snov-Vitovtchina.

It was a chilly morning. A slight rain sprinkled the gathering in the square. We were dressed in our Sabbath clothes, for if the Germans meant to plunder, it was best to be dressed in our finest, to at least save that from the looting. Families poured out onto the streets and into the marketplace. Armed soldiers and machine guns surrounded us.

I stood with my father and my brothers in the first line. I remember seeing Lolek supporting his elderly mother. He was standing near us; his face was tense and strained. This image of my friend Lolek would have to last me forever.

Within an hour, all the Jews in town were assembled. We pressed against each other, seeking security in the crowd. From a corner of the square, I spotted a young woman with a child in her arms. The woman could barely walk; obviously, she had dragged herself from a sick bed. She walked slowly. A German soldier suddenly appeared at her side. With surprising tenderness he took hold of her arm with one hand and with the other supported the infant. Gently and with great patience, he lead her on. He knew he was leading her to death.

The German commandant began to call out people's names according to their trade. Then, from the group of artisans gathered before him, he chose a few, and, with a motion of his finger, directed them to go to the right. The rest he sent back to the group. The artisans did not know which would be better—to be chosen or not. Would they be sent to a camp if chosen, and perhaps have a means of escape? Would remaining at home mean that one would be safer? They had no choice in the matter, however, and the German officer continued singling out artisans: laundry owners, textile workers, tailors, blacksmiths, and tanners.

At the call for carpenters, my father, my brothers and I were directed to the right. We were fortunate not to be separated from each other; we hoped this was a good sign. In all, 585 artisans and professional Jews were transported from the marketplace to the courtyard of the Gymnasium. Among the artisans in our group were Siomka and Fraidel and several of my other comrades. We did not know what our fate would be. The rest were lead out of town.

Shortly afterward, a German soldier came to the Gymnasium and selected a few people for work detail. Zelda Damessek was one of those chosen. Later she related this story: "We were ordered to board a truck which was parked near the Gymnasium. When we crossed to the other side of the marketplace, we realized that the driver was taking us to the square at Radzivil's palace. Along the road, on both sides, we saw Jews, our friends and families, marching under the guard of German soldiers.

"A short distance from the church, the truck came to a halt, and it was impossible to pass. Jews were being marched down the middle of the road, silent and passive. We could hear the bitter crying of an infant complaining of hunger. He had eaten nothing at all since he was taken from his cradle, early that morning. One of the soldiers became annoyed at the infant for breaking the silence. He began to curse.

"I am short and could see nothing of what was happening, but I heard the people standing about me say, 'The German has seized the child.' And after a moment, 'He has choked him!' The crying stopped abruptly. A shudder passed through us all. The terror in our hearts mounted as our hopes retreated. After a short delay, the column of people moved ahead, turning down another street. Our truck was free to pass. When we reached the palace, we were told to clean the rooms and halls; then, we were returned to the Gymnasium.

"About four thousand Jews were taken that day from the square and put to death—two thousand along the road to Snov and two thousand near the Radzivil palace. The children, shot dead or half dead, were thrown into a special pit while their parents were forced to watch. Then the Germans tossed grenades into the pit.

"An old Jew who remained alive said that the skies, at that moment, turned cloudy and dark, for 'The Lord Almighty hid himself so that he might not see and might not hear the murder of his children.'

"Eye witnesses, farmers who were ordered to dig ditches along the road to catch the streams of blood, saw the earth covering the slaughtered tremble."

The day after we were confined to the Gymnasium, the order was given: within four hours, everyone was to move into the ghetto. As we left the Gymnasium building, most of the local non-Jewish population were standing by the road. A few were moved by what they saw. Some were ashamed to face us; their eyes were full of tears. Then there were the rest who stood either with indifference or with obvious joy at our trial. Near my house at the corner, stood my neighbor, Mishlitzki, a former Gymnasium student. When he saw me, he began to whistle cheerfully. That sound cut into my flesh. It still echoes in my ears today.

Jews were running back and forth with small carts, trying to transfer necessary clothes and utensils within the few hours given us. I ran with my father to my uncle's house near the synagogue. We were going to help move my aunt, the wife of the slaughtered Reb Aaron Levine, and my grandmother. My aunt was ill and my grandmother very old. We carried my aunt to her new cramped quarters. We could not find my grandmother. We found out later that she was murdered by the Germans. She must have been over a hundred years old, learned and well tempered. Until her last day, she gave all her attention and love to her children, her grandchildren, and her great-grandchildren.

Within twenty-four hours, everyone was crammed into the few houses that comprised the Nesvizh ghetto. The ghetto was concentrated in the synagogue area, a few tumble down houses surrounded by barbed wire. We were stunned by our new circumstances and by the *Aktion* of the day before. Those who grieved for their lost families went about like living dead, *vie lebedike meysim*.

Squads were organized to collect property from the Jewish houses outside the ghetto and to transfer them to German warehouses. I was picked for one squad. When I touched dear articles of my friends and my family with my own hands, I told myself, "This is a nightmare! This can't be real! Please, no!" But the nightmare continued.

In the evening, shivering with cold, I would hurry along from work in the direction of the ghetto gate. On the way, I'd spot bits of paper, photographs, and letters, scattered by the wind from the opened, ransacked Jewish homes. I'd stop for a moment, quickly pick up a picture, look at it passionately and thrust it into my pocket, a last tangible fragment of the past. And then, even faster, I'd hurry on to my new quarters.

One of the most revolting jobs in the ghetto was burying corpses. One day I was sent, along with a group of Jews, to Glinishtze to bury seven slaughtered Russian soldiers. When I returned, I was sick and numb.

Toward the end of December 1941, I assembled the older members of the underground who had survived, Siomka and Hedva among them. At this meeting we reviewed the situation in the ghetto after the selection, stressing the dangers of self-delusion. The memory of October 30 permeated the ghetto like dense smoke. It choked us. It slowly suffocated us without mercy. We spoke of fighting back. Although we did not formulate a plan, we agreed unanimously that October 30 would not repeated. We would not go meekly to the slaughter.

The situation demanded organization and action. We expanded the ranks of the underground. We inducted Yerahmiel Shklar, who had been a member of *Gordonia;* Bornstein, who was from *Poalei Zion* and a refugee; Nathan Messer, a member of the movement who had come from the Rovno Training Center, also a refugee; and Buzhin, an active Communist who became Jewish once again, with strong, redefined national ideologies.

The central aims of the underground were acquiring arms and establishing contacts outside the ghetto. We began to plan for an internal revolt and for a subsequent flight to the forests to join the partisans against the Germans.

We concentrated on collecting steel—knives, and the like—and we cautiously approached possible contacts who might help us obtain other kinds of arms.

From the Kozimir Synagogue, where I worked with my father and my brother Zhame, I would sneak across to my old house where a young Pole and his mother lived. This fellow had an underground radio. It was in "his" house that I heard outside news. It was with him that we discussed how to obtain weapons. He was a good contact and friend. Soon he was caught by the Germans and executed.

With the coming of winter, I secretly organized a school in the ghetto, despite German regulations against it. Polatchuk, Rechtman, Litevkova, and I taught. Children of very young age would come to the houses of the teachers and study there. We taught each child how to be cautious of the Germans. They also learned reading, writing, geography, arithmetic, and the history of our people. I told and retold legends of the destruction of the Temple, about the "Scroll of Fire," *Kid-*

dush Hashem during the massacres by the Crusaders in 1096, about the Jews in Christian Spain and Czarist Russia, and about Jewish dreamers and fighters. I cherished those meetings with the children.

In a small, dusky room in my house, I taught these young Jewish children. The innocence of childhood and the great maturity gained from suffering were reflected in their dark eyes. I could not ease their pain, but at least I taught them to know that within each one of them was a great light of hope, only temporarily obscured by this present state of darkness. Never had I such an audience. They absorbed everything with overwhelming desire and interest. And each time we parted, I would think sadly that maybe this would be our last meeting.

Life in the ghetto soon became routine, without incident. Once again, delusions grew. We falsely hoped that October 30 was meant to strike terror, to destroy the power to resist and the will to live. This current reprieve fostered new hopes, allowing us to dream of what could be. The Germans carried out no further operations. We let our guard down. There were only two Jewish victims during the first months of the ghetto. Yehoshua Kravitz was caught collecting a debt from a peasant, and the attorney, Messita, was arrested for lingering at the home of a Christian friend outside the ghetto.

This apparent respite could not prepare us for our imminent reckoning.

In addition to reorganizing the resistance to strengthen the ghetto community for revolution, it was vital to undermine Maghalief's position as chairman of the *Judenrat*. His methods were unscrupulous. He believed that bribery alone would ward off calamity, and since he was our only representative to the German command, he had to be stripped of his power.

How could this be done? Members of the underground suggested that since the ghetto was comprised of artisans, it should be the artisans' privilege to determine procedures.

Consequently, we decided that it was necessary to elect an Executive Committee of the Trade Unions to represent the artisans, and it would be incumbent upon the *Judenrat* to accept the Executive's decisions and considerations. Upon approval of this idea, elections were held and an Executive chosen. The Executive consisted mainly of members of the underground, among them Messer, Bornstein, Goldberg, Siomka, Hedva, Yerahmiel, and myself. We were now in a position to restrict Maghalief's authority. Just as important, the underground gained influence throughout the community. The reaction to the creation of the Executive was positive, both within the ghetto and among most of the inhabitants of the town, who also did not want the fate of the ghetto to be in Maghalief's hands.

One of the first steps taken by the Executive Committee was to demand that Maghalief give testimony concerning his part in the events leading up to the October 30 massacre. Maghalief attempted to submit evidence proving his innocence of any complicity. He was on the stand for several hours and was under great strain and anxiety throughout the thorough cross-examination by the Executive. Though he could not be tried and convicted as in a real court of law, his humiliating ordeal was a great moral victory for the underground. The executive made practical demands toward the betterment of ghetto conditions, such as improving the daily distribution of food and increasing the size of the care packages. The demands were met.

The winning over of public opinion and the preparations for defense marked a most important achievement for us all. The underground was aware that an uprising in the small ghetto, even if we succeeded in obtaining arms, would only be possible if there was a total, unified, and active resistance on the part of the entire ghetto, and by the young people in particular. There existed another underground movement in the ghetto, comprised of several young men. As a result of the successes of the executive, these good men, Berl Alperovitz, Moshe Damessek, and Polatschuk among them, were won over and joined with us to form a stronger, more unified fighting force.

Dear G.,

Nights when I am unable to sleep, I find myself "writing" to you in my mind. It is now very late. I am sitting in the little kitchen of our makeshift house. The faint light of the kerosene lamp flickers across the table. The family has been in bed for hours. Tonight, I feel the need to put my thoughts together, to tell you something of what we are going through.

It is the month of April, 1942; it was *Pesach* a few days ago. The ghetto has been in existence for half a year, though it seems as if it has been a lifetime. I cannot imagine that outside this place, people are unaware of what is going on. And yet we have heard no reaction or response from anyone. Can it be possible for things like this to occur with no help in sight?

About four thousand Jews in our town were put to death in an *Aktion* on October 30, the year nineteen hundred and forty one. They were massacred. I cannot find the strength to tell you about the day. I do not know whether you can comprehend such a thing happening. I am still unable to do so.

Afterwards, we were ordered to collect, from the houses of our slaughtered Jews, their clothing and property for distribution among the Germans. The next day we were sent to the warehouse to sort out piles of clothing. Some of us recognized clothes of brothers and sisters, of relatives. Every now and then, there would be a chilling cry of anguish, "Oy, it's Chayimke's!" or "It's Sarale's!"

Ordered to gather useful articles, I had entered Yaroshevitz's house, where Shaul Friedstein had lived before the selection. There were already signs of plundering. I recognized articles of clothing and furniture. Suddenly I came upon some photographs of Shaul, his wife Bella, and their lovely little daughter Na'ava. They were scattered across the floor, these pictures of frozen smiles. I wanted to take them all back home with me, but I knew there would be no way of hiding them. Instead, I selected one picture, of Shaul dressed as the *Yid Zeiss*, and hid it in my coat. While I was passing through Sirokomala Street opposite Katchenovski's house, I spotted discarded papers and pictures; they were frayed and had been soiled by the rain. I bent down and picked up a photo of Bomka and Dubba taken in the orchard of Kibbutz Elon. This was the very picture I had seen at the home of Bomka's parents in the summer of 1939. I slipped it into my pocket. And so I began to collect pictures of a life that used to be.

The ghetto has the form of a *yud* about 150 meters wide and 250 meters long. In it is a handful of frame houses and five brick synagogues, including the Kalte Shul. A fence encircles us from the corner of Sirokomala Street to the corner of Mikhalishok Street. From there it goes up the middle of the street to an alley called the *toyte gessel*. The alleyways I remember from my childhood. Although I lived in the suburb of the town of Kozimir, I would walk through them on my way from *cheder* in the Ladeier Shul, holding my kerosene lantern. On winter nights, I was wrapped in warm clothing with a *bashlik* on my head. In the Kalte Shul I had studied in the *Talmud Torah* with my first teacher, Moshe Yudelvitz. And at the *Tiferet Bachurim,* I would be tested weekly on passages of the *Gemorrah*. How distant all this seems now.

Only a few complete families have been saved; most have lost members. And there are scattered survivors, alone with only the company of memories. From where do they draw the spiritual strength to go on?

A tree grows in our ghetto. It is the only one. It is near our house. With spring, it burst into bloom as if in defiance of all things ugly. And then it withered. More than anything else, it reminds me of the passing of life.

There is also a garden in the ghetto. Along the last five or six houses down Mikhalishok Street, there is a strip of land. Several famlies have cultivated the soil and planted cucumbers, lettuce, radishes, and onions. Even this spot of green in the ghetto saddens us with memories of what was.

A few weeks ago, toward evening, on my way back from work, I met Tfardoklebov, my nature study instructor at the Polish *Gymnasium*. He recognized me though his face was set in a frozen look of indifference. By now I have come to recognize this look, not as one of unconcern, but one of guilt from an obvious delight at our plight. Tfardoklebov had not approved of the Jews teaching in the Polish *Gymnasium* during the Soviet occupation. What was happening to us now was adequate revenge for him.

At present I am working with Neufeld as a carpenter in the Radzivil Palace. Neither of us is professional, and we dread each assignment lest we fail. At dawn every morning, Neufeld and I leave the ghetto, cross the marketplace, and walk past the church, the iron portal, and the long avenue of lilacs and chestnut trees that bloom along both sides of the road. The avenue is half visible through the rising fog. On the right is the large lake of the Radzivils. A cool morning breeze blows across the lake. Across the lake are lovely small houses. To the left of the road stretch meadows of colorful wild flowers, purple, white, and yellow. In spite of our heavy spirits, we cannot resist being touched by the magic of the scene before us. Not far away are the pits filled with slaughtered Jews. After work, Neufeld and I walk back to the ghetto in the light of the setting sun.

Thanks to our connections, we have not gone hungry. Food is limited, but sufficient. We smuggle in some flour, barley, and, occasionally, some fat. My brother Motele, the talented mathematician, has also become a proficient

63

homemaker; he cooks soup and bakes bread.

During the first days of the ghetto, I secretly went out with Father one evening to visit a Christian neighbor, an acquaintance. We asked him to exchange some of our clothes for food. He agreed. From time to time, we enjoy his assistance. He takes a fee for his role as an agent, but the extra food is too vital for any quibbling. Volodka, the Polish teacher, also helps us. She lives on the hill, a few hundred meters from our house. During the Russian period, we worked together at the school. The Soviet authorities regarded her with suspicion since she was a Pole. My comrades and I were friendly with her. Several times she has placed a small parcel of food by the barbed wire fence near our house. I have such a feeling of respect and gratitude for this good-hearted woman. Will I ever be able to repay her for her good deeds?

When I meet Tomako, the Polish geography teacher, he always removes his hat and bows deeply. This open act of defiance against the Germans sustains the hope within me that there are still good moral people in the world. A certain friendship has sprung up between us since my appearance at the teacher's meeting, so long ago, when I defended the right of Shaul Friedstein, the Zionist, to be elected as a member of the Nesvizh Teachers' Committee. When he met me the following day, he shook my hand warmly and with respect. He is a fine person, a humanitarian, with a deep attachment to Polish romantic literature and poetry. He has a profound feeling for a suffering people.

But these stories of kindness are isolated cases. They do not overshadow the cultivated hatred that grows so bountifully outside our ghetto fence. A short time ago, a group of Jews were transported to work in Kletsk. As our vehicle came to a halt, we saw a man running toward us, shouting and cursing, his arms waving with clenched fists. He ran around the car like a madman, spewing his venom at us. I asked myself how could one human being accumulate such hatred? By order of the German guard riding with us, our protector, we continued on our way just in time.

Aunt Chaya Levine, the late Reb Levine's wife, passed away two months ago. My father and I had carried her from her sick bed to this ghetto, and she died in a strange room. We took care of her all this time, and when she questioned, "Where is my husband, where is Aaron?," we told her that he must have been arrested. She died not knowing that Reb Levine was murdered by our captors. The neighbors consoled themselves at her funeral, "At least she died without that knowledge of the horrible truth; at least she is buried in a Jewish grave."

My brothers and my father and I are fortunate that we have remained together with the coming of the Germans, and yet, this fills me with sadness and dread. I had such hope that at least one of us would make it to *Eretz*. At least one! I thought that Zhame would be the lucky one; after all, he was in Vilna, so close to the border. If he had made it, continuation of our heritage would have been assured. Now that we are all together, we are destined to share the same fate, whatever that may be. This oppressive feeling of being together will not leave me. I do not discuss it with my brothers.

Many times a day the mood of the Jews in the ghetto changes. I enter the home of L. or G. or N. and find them apathetic, lost in thought. In their thoughts, in their every movement, death stalks: "The Jews will be annihilated!" And then, without apparent reason, dim hope gleams once more. "Perhaps we will outlive this, and we will soon live again in freedom. Even in the shadow of death, hope will not abandon us."

A piece of good news reaches the ghetto; eyes begin to sparkle. "The Russians have taken over, maybe redemption is in the offing." And then imaginations run rampant. Arguments and discussions flare: "Will there be a quick German retreat? Will they have time to liquidate the few Jews still remaining in the ghettos? There is no doubt that the Russians, with their inexhaustible reserves, are preparing themselves for crushing counterattacks. And the U.S. is helping, too. The U.S.! That means the whole world against the Germans! They'll make mincemeat out of them. The Germans are already beginning to feel the pinch. Why, I heard the German work supervisor at the Radzivil Palace sum up the situation as *"nicht gut, nicht gut."* Soon the enthusiasm dies down and everyone becomes somber. "But where are the Russians? Where is the United States?"

A few months back, I visited M., who was living in the last house on Sirokomala Street. It had been a cold, snowy day. There was frost. The time was just before evening. The glowing red sunset glimmered in the narrow room where we sat. M., a refugee from western Poland, had been my pupil during the Soviet occupation. He was depressed and agitated, rising from his chair, pacing, and sitting once again. He spoke, seemingly unaware that I was present: "On our graves, I should like a tall monument with a great torch reaching to the skies. And on it, in great letters of fire, there shall be engraved, "Thousands of Jews Were Massacred on This Spot by the German Nazis." And after the war, everyone traveling by the Continental Express between Paris and Moscow through Horodzei will see this monument."

He raved on and on until it seemed that his strength was gone, and then collapsed exhausted on his bed. I slipped out of the house quietly. With sudden anger and conviction, I said to myself that may be his last word, but it won't be mine.

A while back, a peasant told my brother Zhame that he had heard stories of roaming partisans in the area. If this were true, we wondered why they haven't contacted us. Nevertheless, the drive to fight and escape is becoming intense. We disregard the overwhelming odds, and concentrate on plans. We must reinforce the fighting units so that most of the population, women and children, can escape and flee to the forest six kilometers away. More and more Jews are identifying with the underground, even the older ones like Moshe Reuben Zaturenski and Klattchko.

Obtaining firearms is still a problem. We have begun equipping outselves with substitutes, rods, knives, irons, chemical acids, anything that we can use as weapons. Leah Dukkar and Rachel Kagan smuggled a machine gun, part by part, from the German arsenal where they work.

Our spirit is fierce and strong. One member of the underground, Michael O., expresses our feelings in poetry:

Do not rejoice, beasts of prey.
Do not dream of feasts and drink.
Do not look forward and do not prepare yourselves
To lead a people to its doom.
A day will come.
Indeed it is nearer now,
Standing proudly behind our wall,
When in waves the people will rise
And revenge the blood that has been spilled.

Until the full story is known, we will never understand why the outside world has not come to our aid, why our suffering and anguish have not been heard. Don't they know that it is their pain, too? Who can say whether some faint echo of us will remain, whether our names will be drowned forever in our unheeded cries. But I do know that no matter what our chances of success are or whether we receive any help from the outside, we will fight to overcome and survive.

S.

On July 17, 1942, we heard the news of the extermination of the Jews of the Horodzei ghetto, fourteen kilometers away. The news struck our ghetto like a bolt of lightning. All delusions dissolved. What we did not know then was that this was no isolated incident. A wave of slaughter had already wiped out Jewish ghettoes in White Russia and the Ukraine.

On that day, we, the Jews of the Nesvizh ghetto, gathered at the new synagogue. The congregation stood still as death. The *Kaddish* was spoken. Silent anguish gave way to moaning, to choked tears. Our grief was for those fallen Jews. Or did each person sense that the congregation was reciting *Kaddish* for itself?

At the memorial meeting, I rallied the mourners: "Fellow Jews! We are isolated and cut off from the Jewish world, from the world at large. It may be that not a word of our plight has been heard. It may be that we are the last of the ghettoes and the last of the Jews. We must fight for our lives! We shall defend the ghetto, the place of suffering. We will fight as would the last remaining Jews on the soil of their homeland. We will prepare, now, to strike. We will be on the alert. The right moment may come at any time!"

The entire population of the ghetto was with us. Last minute arrangements were concluded. A plan of attack was finalized: As soon as the Germans advanced and surrounded the ghetto, a pile of straw would be ignited near the synagogue. The fighting groups would set fire to assigned houses, thereby directing the battle towards the forest, our cover. All would flee there. Toward evening on July 20, I divided the youth and all those capable of fighting into units of five. They were assigned to posts by Hirschel Svitski, one of our strategists. Fordes, the chemist, and Goldberg distributed acid preparations. Yisrael Shusterman and Yosef Langman portioned out liters of gasoline and kerosene. Our only machine gun was set up in the great synagogue, in the women's section. Aharel Goch would be the gunner.

Nobody left the ghetto. Buzhin, the former Communist, pondered sending his eight-year-old daughter to one of his non-Jewish friends, but at the end he decided against it: "I do not want my daughter to grow up and be a *goyah*."

68

The suspense was great, the ghetto sensitive to every possible sign to attack.

We waited.

At dusk, the ghetto was suddenly surrounded by Belorussian police. I hurried to meet with Nathan Messer and Siomka Farfel to make sure that everything was set.

I went home to gather up final possessions, family pictures, a photograph of my mother, some letters and notes, and a knife. I embraced my father and my brothers. I still remember the parting words of my brother as we held each other: "Ich vill zei dem gorgel zebiessen" ("I will cut their throats to bits"). I choked back my tears and left to regroup with my comrades.

The underground leadership sat up all night, tensely waiting reports of a new German movement. At dawn on July 21, 1942, the police shot their way into the home of Damessek and fatally wounded his wife. The fighting units scattered to their designated positions. The rest of the Jews ran to the ghetto gate. Maghalief arrived at the gate to inform us that the German commandant had ordered an immediate selection. Only essential artisans, first and foremost thirty textile workers without their families, would remain alive.

The members of the underground and the mass of Jews standing at the gate replied resolutely, "No! There will be no selection! If some are to live, then all must; if not, we shall defend ourselves!"

Maghalief returned to the German commandant with our answer. The Germans opened fire. The fighting unit in the synagogue answered with a surprise volley of machine gun fire. The Germans crashed through the ghetto gate. The Jews drew their knives and irons. They reached for their pile of stones. I saw a group of Jews attack a charging German and kill him. Klattchko, an older man, and Yisrael Shusterman battled with one of the policemen and knocked him dead. The Germans increased their firing. A battle began between

69

Jews with steel weapons and Germans and police with guns. More skirmishes, hand to hand combat, shooting.

Soon the ghetto was filled with dead and dying. Throughout the streets, bodies lay like discarded puppets. The Jews set fire to their houses. The flames spread quickly towards the center of the town. A horde of local peasants from the outlying neighborhood swarmed into the ghetto, plundering before all was devoured by the fire. The madness of their pillaging and the fury of the Germans to kill matched the frenzy of every Jew, man, woman, child, to flee from the burning ghetto. People were running, screaming, crying. I went to check the various fighting posts and then returned to my position. Siomka Farfel, Shmuel Nissenbaum, and I were caught in a volley of gunfire at the post where I was stationed. We jumped into an underground bunker at Anuteshnik's house. After a few moments we escaped to the attic. There we lay on the floor with knives in hand, facing the ladder, the only access to the attic. A group of Germans entered the house. One of them took hold of the ladder, shook it, and began to go up. We held our breath, set to strike. Suddenly, another soldier called to the one climbing, "We already looked the place over, let's go." The soldier hesitated and then went down the ladder. They left.

From the attic we could see crowds of non-Jews with arms full of clothes and goods, wildly jumping and jeering whenever a Jew was shot. We remained in the attic until we were able to sneak out. We ran south through the alleys, circled the city, crossed the Nesvizh-Horodzei Road, and entered the fields of grain.

Small groups of Jews like ours burst forth from the ghetto. Once outside, some were beaten by zealous peasants. Others were killed in flight. Small groups succeeded in reaching the forest. I saw Simcha Rozen carrying his small son wrapped in a pillow. As Simcha ran, he passed the bundle to a Christian woman standing near the gate and then continued running towards the woods.

70

As I ran from the ghetto all I could think of was that we Jews of Nesvizh had revolted against the Germans! A community of Jews cut off and isolated from any outside contact had arisen. We were a small community, but one that embraced all the sufferings and all the hopes of a people. We had become one fighting group. We had succeeded in overcoming the Germans and the police. I later learned that the Nesvizh ghetto was the first ghetto to revolt against the Nazis.

In the dim light of dawn, the charred ghetto was gray. Heaps of ruined buildings smouldered. Little flames flickered above the glowing ashes, appropriate remembrance candles for those buried beneath. Only they will remain there, mute witnesses to our suffering and courage. I took one last look at the burning ghetto, took one deep breath of the scorched air, and went on with my comrades into the forest.

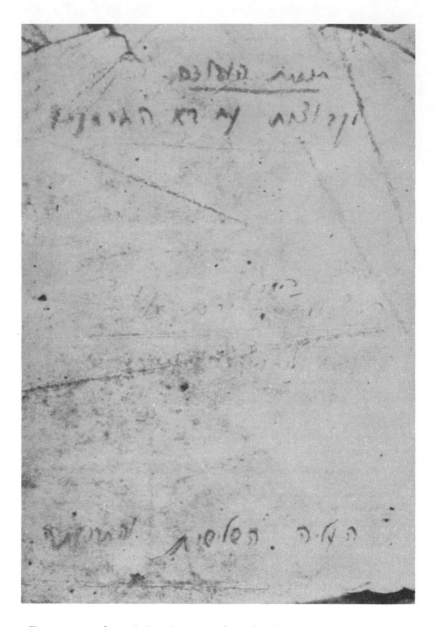

Fragments of work book soon after the German occupation of Nesvizh.

72

List of students in the clandestine school in the Nesvizh Ghetto, handwritten by the teacher Polatchuk.

IV группа

1. Маргалин
2. Резник
3. Ротлеви
4. Найфельд
5. Горузель
6. Бельчинский
7. Карон
8. Цинкович

Препод.: Полячек

1. Абрамович
2. Гинзбург
3. Лиговска
4. Резник
5. Шабес
6. Абрамович

Препод. Рехтман

I группа
1. Марковский
2. Могилев

Препод.: Гальдитки

II. группа
1. Эрлихевич
2. Маргалин
3. Лишин
4. Басинкевич
5. Холявский
6. Рутштейн

2. Зубак Лейб
3. Ранд Мирия
4. Гринвальд ...
1933 г.

III. группа
1. Ре...
2. Холявска

1. Берлинер Зин
2. Вельчинский ...
3. Шиманович
1932 г.

3+

Неявочные всеобучем или
отсеялись (по годам):

1935 г.
1. Рим Люба
2. Найдель Лея
1934 г.
1. Воловянская Ля...

группы

1. Бослявянска Л.

2. Лабес Л.

3. Робак А.

⎫
⎬ Преподаватель
⎭ Литвако.

II группа

1. Маргалин

2. Шабес

3. Липовский

4. Давидовский

Крейнов.

III группа

1. Кишивицкий

2. Розенберг

3. Янкелевич

4. Бассин

5. Абрамович

6. Бухер.

Mass graves of the Jewish martyrs of Nesvizh.

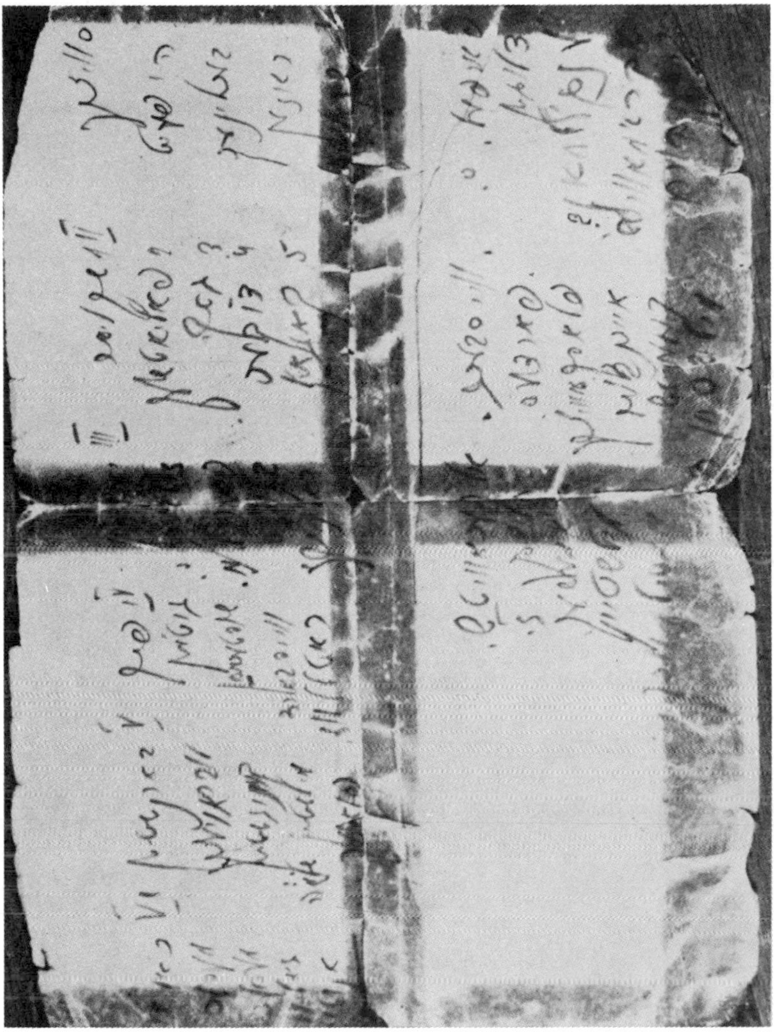

Part Three

On the second day of the uprising and our escape the three of us, Siomka, Shmuel, and I, sought shelter at a farmer's house in Vinkelerovstchina, a village near Nesvizh. As the farmer offered us a bit of food, he said, "The Jews of Nesvizh showed what they can do. The town is almost completely burned to the ground. There are dead and wounded Germans and police everywhere." What he was saying hardly penetrated our consciousness. All that had taken place within the past few days we could not absorb. We were stunned and tired. Just to gather berries, our only source of food during our wanderings, made us dizzy. We had to drag ourselves from bush to bush in order to eat.

As we came close to the edge of the forest, we met a group of peasant women carrying scythes. They were returning from the fields. At the sight of us, they screamed and began to flee, crying in terror like a flock of geese. We learned later that they were afraid we would abuse them and then ruthlessly cut out their tongues. The Germans had spread rumors that the escaping Jews were madmen, ready and willing to rape and kill. We were amazed at their reaction, but grateful that no encounter took place.

The following day at dawn, we came upon a young shepherdess. At first she recoiled, but then, regaining some courage, she yelled at us as she turned to run, "You may succeed in surviving a week, but no matter. The Germans will kill you anyway." Again, we were shaken by this kind of reaction. We did not look menacing; we were weak and hungry and afraid of our destiny.

It was quiet in the fields and woods, and yet not soothing. There was tension in the air, a suspense that urged us to keep alert. We could hear gunfire echoing occasionally in the distance. We did not know who was shooting, and all we could guess was that either Jews were being shot or partisans were battling the Germans. Rumors from peasants of a battle between the Germans and the partisans in the nearby village of Rayuvka gave us hope for the latter.

We began to hear of groups of Jews who had succeeded in getting out of towns such as Nesvizh, Kletsk, and Lakhovitz, which was situated to the west of the former Polish-Russian border, and from Kopyl and Timkovitzi to the east. The groups were heading in the direction of the forests in the Kopyl region. A wave of exterminations swept through these towns in the month of July 1942. Fate seemed to bring the fleeing Jews together. Those coming out of the western ghettoes had an intuitive feeling that there were partisans in the region and that they were camped somewhere to the east of the border. Friendly peasants we met pointed the way for us: "Go eastward."

In the Kopyl region, we met up with the Meierovitz-Geller group who escaped from Kletsk, and Yosef Pecker's group from Lakhovitz. Simcha Rozen and and Michael Fish, who had escaped from the Nesvizh ghetto, happily joined our group.

Bands of Jews wandered about in surrounding forests searching for a sign of the partisans. The wandering was filled with danger. Many peasants spying on us from the fields would demand payment for their silence. Only in the Soviet zone did we feel safe. The villagers of Yavishtza were friendly to partisans and Jews. They would supply us with cooked food and foodstuffs.

Rachel Filler, who fled from Vishkov to Timkovitzi and then to Kopyl with her son, told a story that typified what happened to many of us:

"After I left the bunker in Timkovitzi with my boy, we wandered in the forests, frightened by every sound and movement. I had only a bundle of clothes with me. One day, as we were walking, a peasant suddenly jumped out from the bushes. We were startled and froze where we stood. He asked, 'Who are you?'

"In that split second, a thousand answers rushed into my head. What should I tell him? What was less dangerous? Finally I said, 'I am crazy!'

" 'If you say so,' the peasant replied, 'most probably you're not. You are fleeing from the Germans. Why don't you join the partisans?'

" 'I haven't a gun,' I said.

"Then he smiled: 'I have a gun. What do you have in exchange for it?'

"I was afraid he was going to rob me. I said nothing. He told us to wait for him to return in ten minutes, and with that he was gone. I was sure that he was going to bring the Germans. I said to my boy, 'Let's run away.' But then I reconsidered. How many Germans did he need to finish me off? If that was what he meant to do, he certainly could have done it already, by himself, without any help. A few minutes later, the peasant returned with an axe in his hand. I began to shake, my teeth chattering. 'Be calm,' He whispered. Then he went over to a tree and struck it several times with the axe. Reaching into a hole in the tree, he pulled out a gun and gave it to me. I didn't know how to thank him. As I left, he also gave me food and supplies. I gave him a jacket and several meters of cloth. He was my delivering angel.

"Because of the gun, when I finally did reach a group of partisans, I was accepted into their ranks. That gun was among the first acquired by the unit."

Although most of us experienced similar support, we were still wary of people who claimed to be our "saviors." It was too easy to turn us in for a bag of salt or a liter of kerosene.

A unit of Russian partisans was encamped in Rayuvka. It was made up of local people, Red Army soldiers who were hidden by peasants during the winter, and those who had escaped from prison camps. With the coming of spring they banded together in the forest; they were few in number and poorly armed. After two or three months, the unit increased, and by the time the Jews came in July of that year, there were seventy or eighty in all. It was a small unit, but its territory of influence extended to many villages and towns in the direction of Minsk to the north, to the Polish swamps in the south, and to the Naliboki forests on the west. Its combat squads reached distant regions, and as they passed through an area, they created the impression that they were strong and well armed. These units were a constant topic of conversation among the peasants, who would whisper that large Soviet forces were moving about in the area.

It did not take long for the partisans to establish a firm contact with the population, displaying that all important pretense that they were an organized, disciplined, and powerful body. The ambush of a German military convoy in the second half of July in Rayuvka brought a great victory to the partisans. It was the largest and worst defeat the Germans garrison suffered in that region. The battle lasted more than six hours. Over thirty-five Germans were killed or wounded; losses to the partisans were slight. It put the German army to shame. Most important, the victory inspired the local population and brought them closer to the partisans.

Although the Germans were positioned on the road to the Caucasus and in the regions of Leningrad and Moscow during the summer of 1942, the partisans began to make appearances in the nearby villages of Lavi, Yavishtza, and Yazvina. Indeed, when the partisan guardsmen appeared mounted on elegant horses, wearing parts of military uniforms with *kubankas* and red stars, and riding boldly through the village, they were a splendid sight for the peasants and for the boys and girls in the town. Even the requisition of food from the peasants did not undo the relationship; the peasants knew that the partisans were more civilized than the Germans. When the partisans took fresh food and meat from farms supervised by the Germans and worked by the peasants, the burden of taxes for the farmers was lightened.

The unit continued to grow and, in time, split into several groups—the Dunayev, Yarominko, Shestopavlov, and others. Later they regrouped to form a brigade under the leadership of Major General Kapusta.

In July 1941, Kapusta was badly wounded in the leg during a skirmish. He was captured. As a prisoner in the camp, he gathered a group of men with the intention of escaping and organizing a band of partisans. In the spring of 1942, Kapusta and his prisoner comrades escaped to the Staritza forests. They numbered fourteen; among them was one Jew, Zuvarayev. In the forest, they were joined by another Jew, Gilchik from Kopyl. Zuvarayev and Gilchik excelled, the former as a scout and the latter as an officer. After the success of the first battles, the unit became famous, and many Jews came to join up with the fighting group.

The day we made our way to the camp, Kapusta appeared, accompanied by one of his comrades. The leader was a man of forty years, tall and sturdy. He had a strong body, though one of his hands was bandaged and held in a sling. He had been wounded, as we learned afterwards, in the battle of Rayuvka which had taken place a few days before. An old scar beneath his forehead added character to the face of this veteran fighter. Kapusta possessed self-confidence, and we saw in him one who had not compromised his soul in the muddy stream of the times. His appearance both stirred and encouraged us. He asked from which ghettoes we had escaped and why we had lingered so long in coming to his camp.

In all we numbered about forty in the forest; the Jewish base was about a kilometer from that of the other partisans.

In general, there were no difficulties in enlisting Jews who had reached the forest. Girls and women, however, who looked Aryan and could be suspected of espionage were interrogated most severely. After the investigation, they were attached to our camp. The Jewish base was composed mainly of young males, though it included a number of girls and some older people from the district of Kopyl. Weiner, a party member from Kopyl, and therefore trustworthy in the eyes of the Russians, was appointed provisional commander of the base.

During the first days, a number of shelters were set up and a temporary kitchen was organized. We were able to restore our strength with food served in unlimited quantities. Meat was brought in and freely distributed. At night we would ride to the nearby villages and take white cheese and eggs from the peasants. After so many days of hunger and want, these delicacies gave new life to our bodies.

Everyone kept to themselves, sleeping most of the day or at least trying to sleep anyway. Our clothes smelled of the ghetto, and we could not forget the madness of our flight. What brought us closer together was the campfire at night. The fire revived our spirits, warmed our hearts, and instilled a feeling of closeness. The youngsters, wrapped in blankets and sitting around the fire, would dry green tobacco leaves on forked branches, turning them over until the leaves would be completely dry and brown. Then they would crumple the leaves by the handful and pour the crumbs into a piece of paper cut from newspapers. After rolling and pasting, they would have the classic partisan cigrette. It would be about four inches long and thicker than a usual cigarette. Each of us would take a drag. While smoking and passing the cigarette, we exchanged stories, which would lead to new acquaintances. Although there was quite a difference between the Jews of the West and those of the East, there was no real division between them. Our common fate was stronger than any difference. In these

88

short snatches of conversations, we found the opportunity to release the unresolved terror from which we had fled.

One night a number of us were sitting by the fire. A few had already retired for the night. Those lying beneath the pine trees had made pillows of grass and had covered themselves with the only piece of clothing they had managed to salvage. Some of the more ambitious ones had already succeeded in erecting forest shelters from branches. Although the covering was frail, the shelter did create a certain feeling of "home." The dry twigs crackled in the fire, breaking the heavy stillness. Before us sat a girl aged seventeen, blonde and pale. Rachel was her name and this was her story:

"A year ago, in October, most of the Jews of Kletsk were slaughtered. My parents were killed then. There remained some fifteen hundred Jews in the ghetto. At times I worked in the ghetto, and sometimes in the fields harvesting potatoes. We were free to move from village to village then, and, remembering my aunt in Hantchevitz, I wrapped my head in a kerchief and headed for her town. On arriving at her house, I found my aunt in shock. Her two children had been slaughtered. There was no alternative for me but to return home.

"At 3:00 on the morning of July 22, the ghetto was surrounded. Kerosene was poured on some of the houses, and the fire spread quickly. We fled in fear and confusion into the streets. My sister and I were near the gate when the Belorussian and German police began shooting. There was a group of Jews with guns, and they returned the fire. Others cried out for help. Some shouted, Dershist mich! (Shoot me!)' Their shouts made the heavens ring. There were Jews who hanged themselves; others hid in bunkers. Suddenly we were pushed by the crowd toward the barbed wire fence. I spotted Yankel Geller, Shmuckler, and Karshezki, my friends.- Someone cut the wire. We were shoved through. A bullet hit my sister and she fell. I began to run wildly, westward. Then suddenly I changed direction and fled eastward. They were chasing me. I lay down flat in a soft field of grain.

"After a time, I got up and ran in the direction of the forest. I passed houses along the way. I entered one of them and told the woman living there that I had fled from Kleck. She received me warmly. She cried terribly at my despair and invited me to stay the night. I refused. She brought me food, told me that my best chance would be with the partisans, and directed me toward the forest. Her husband came back from the fields. 'Maybe you will remain with us,' he said. 'We will adopt you as our daughter.'

"But I didn't want to remain. I wanted to go to the forest. I went in the direction of the Polish-Russian border, crossed the border, and met some laborers in the field. I told them that I wanted to meet up with the partisans. No one paid attention to me. Then an old man came over to me and whispered, 'My son is with the partisans. Come to my house and when my son comes, you can go with him. But for now, wait until the workers leave.'

"I waited until everyone had gone and then went with the old man to his house. I was welcomed kindly. The house was so nicely arranged. It was all so lovely. At the sight of such a serene home, and after having wandered alone and scared for a week, I burst into tears. I thought to myself, 'O God in Heaven, look at me, only a girl—and people are blessed with such a peaceful existence!' "

Rachel paused for a moment, lowering her head; her blonde hair covered her face. She had uttered the last sentence with such despair. The campfire was dying, but the coals glowed in the dark. Someone added a few twigs, but no one else made a move to end the silence. It seemed as if each one of the listeners had been expecting this moment, waiting in dread for someone to tap the flow of thoughts that had been bottled up for such a long time within each of us.

"That night," Rachel continued softly, "I slept in the pea-

90

sant's house. The following day he said, 'Tonight you will sleep in the barn.' Then in the middle of the night, I heard footsteps. I sat up terrified. The old man came. 'We have received an order,' he said. 'Whoever is found hiding a Jew will be shot. You must go. I wanted to do my best. I am sorry. You must escape to the forest.'

" 'But where will I go?' I asked him. He showed me the road. It was a lovely moonlit night. There were some horses grazing in the field. Every shadow scared me to death until at last I came to the forest. I walked on until I was in the village of Savitz. I came to a house, knocked on the door, and went in. The man inside said to me, 'Do you know who I am? I am Soltis.'

"I didn't know who he was, and too exhausted to run, I said to him, 'What do I care. If you want to, hand me over.'

" 'You are too lovely to turn over to the Germans,' he said.

"I fled from the house and continued on into the forest. I sat down to rest. Then I heard steps. I jumped up, ready to run. I heard someone say, 'Rachel?' I turned terrified, and then I was overcome with joy. They were my friends Shmuckler and Fress. Suddenly we heard an exchange of shots. 'It's the Germans!' I cried. We ran and hid in a nearby barn. We waited there for twenty-four hours. When we left the barn, we saw several armed men coming toward us. They looked like partisans. We went over to them happy and trembling, pleading with them to let us join their group. They promised to take us with them if we waited for them at an appointed place. When they returned, they left hastily without taking us along. A shepherd told us that a big battle had taken place yesterday near Rayuvka and that the whole village had gone up in flames. 'Perhaps,' he added, 'the partisans were still in the neighborhood.' He showed us the road to Rayuvka, and we began walking. Soon we spotted a man in a German uniform riding a bicycle.

91

We immediately hid, but we had been spotted. 'Out, right away!' the German shouted.

"I went first. Our captor asked for our papers and took us to the forest. I did not look like a Jewess, so I was investigated. He brought us to Kapusta, who asked, 'And why didn't you bring a gun? Without a gun we won't take you in.' But in the end he agreed."

During its very first days, our group was called upon to participate in raids. A number of unarmed Jewish youngsters were attached to an armed partisan company for a raid on the Sovkhoz farm, which was under German supervision and guard. They were cleaning out its livestock and foodstuffs. The Jewish boys marched along under the cover of partisan guns; they had nothing to defend themselves with in the face of possible fire from the German watch. Nevertheless, that night, herds of cows and pigs were brought into the partisan camp.

The main task of our unit was to acquire firearms. Encouraged by Kapusta, several groups set out in search. Kapusta recommended that they turn toward the former Polish-Russian border where battles had taken place between the German invaders and the Red Army and where there might be arms that had been abandoned by the retreating army. I went together with Rozen, Nissenbaum, and other comrades in the direction of Stolptzi; Meierovitz and his group set out in the direction of Kleck. We were given *otrezs,* which were guns with shortened barrels. We reached the Nieman region near the village of Yazvini, but in the entire area, there were no firearms to be found. It was possible that there had once been arms in the region, but the peasants, who were well acquainted with the forest, must have gathered and hidden them during the time that elapsed since the region was the border, more than a year ago. The Meierovitz group also returned empty-handed.

The partisans were not in the habit of staying in the same forest even when the enemy's eye was not upon them. From time to time we would shift from one forest to another, and soon the encampment moved from Rayuvka to the forest of Vilshin.

The Jewish unit, still in the process of formation, expanded. From the forests in the neighborhood came individuals eager to join. Near the camp several hundred meters away, there was a Jewish family that had settled down after fleeing from Grozovo. It consisted of the Jewish blacksmith, Hershel Sklar, his wife, his old mother-in-law, and three little children. They were the nucleus of what was to become known as the "family camp." Periodically, numbers from the Jewish unit would go over to visit them and bring them food, feeling a deep concern for the little Jewish nest that somehow had been saved. The blacksmith and his family were quiet folks and very amiable. Their ways were simple. They accepted their fate with a certain submission, but without despair, which surprised many. They had an unusual capacity to adapt themselves to conditions of life and locale. The difficulties of the forest did not bring them to a state of bewilderment, but rather to an expression of balance, maturity, and courage.

At the end of August 1942, the Soviet Command appointed Gilchik commander of the Jewish unit. Gilchik was a Russian Jew from Kopyl, and the Soviet command, which was directed by the Communist party, placed more faith in persons originating from the East. Gilchik served as a scout for the partisan command. He had been a resident of Kopyl and had worked as a director of the cattle department in town. In the course of his work, he came in contact with the farmers in the vicinity, and so he knew the territory well. Once, when he returned home from a scouting expedition, he found the German police waiting for him. Gilchik went into hiding, and the Germans took his Christian wife and their two children. Despite the torture they suffered, they did not

93

reveal where Gilchik was hidden. They were shot.

Gilchik succeeded in making his way back to the forest. He was an unaffected person, practical and devoted to his duty. He spoke rarely, but if anyone dared to challenge his Jewishness, he reacted violently. He prided himself on defending his honor. He had come to the encampment equipped with arms.

Gilchik's first order was to obtain more weapons, which, as we were finding out, was not an easy job. The peasants had hidden most of them for their own purposes. Even when several sources confirmed that a particular person had arms, we often had to resort to intense interrogation before the weapons would be handed over.

Before long a piece of news made its way from one of the peasants to the staff. In a certain place in the Kopyl region, a mass grave of Red Army soldiers had been discovered, and it was reportedly filled with weapons. This was in accordance with the Germans' mocking custom of demonstrating their contempt for the Red Army by not deeming it worthwhile to gather up the spoils of war, but instead burying the soldiers with their guns.

We went out that night, a large group of Jewish men with Gilchik in the lead. When we arrived at the spot, we opened the grave and, in the dark, began to pull out, from in between the bodies, the long clumps covered with sticky soil. The terror of death and the guilt of sacrilege enveloped us.

When we returned with the wagon and its load, the news of our success flooded the camp. Some of the men took the clumps of earth and went to work. Using knives, irons, and stones, they began to scrape off the earth that had stuck to the metal parts of the guns. The dirt clung with unyielding strength to what sometimes turned out to be bones. Fires burned throughout the night, and the men worked diligently on through the following day. This night and day did much to shape the fighting character of the Jewish unit. As a result, we had added thirty-five guns to our arsenal. Most of the rifles were ordinary Russian guns, some of them semiautomatic, with a magazine containing ten bullets each. There was one machine gun. After the guns had been cleaned, Siomka Farfel, Shmuel Nissenbaum, Loptitski, and I brought several carpenter's tools from the Vilyshin Kolkhoz, some three or four kilometers from the forest, and we began to fashion stocks for the guns.

Within a few days, most of the men were armed. The unit was recognized as an independent Jewish unit bearing the name of "Zhukov," after the rising star among the commanders of the Red Army, and we were placed under the orders of the partisan command in the Kopyl region, with Kapusta as the leader.

At this point, a remarkable transformation took place. We felt stronger, almost unconquerable. In possession of an instrument for defense and attack, we had absolute control. Only yesterday we were creeping through the fields and villages, dreading every rustle and movement, fearful of the light of day. As an organized fighting group, with these weapons, we were able to leave the forest, on horseback or on foot, with our guns suspended from our shoulders. We could walk about as if we were lords of the same fields where we once groveled. But it was not the arms and the unit alone that made us feel secure and powerful.

The Kapusta Brigade had grown quickly. Because of the skill of its commander, the brigade wielded immense authority throughout the entire region, even stretching to outlying areas. Although most of the new men who reached the forest had come from prison camps, there was among them a nucleus of soldiers instilled with ideals that gave substance to the unit's fighting and social morale. One such fighter was the illustrious partisan commander, Dunayev.

He was a Russian, thirty years of age, blonde, of average height, with an animated face and flaming eyes. He was a supreme fighting commander. His military operations were unique. With small groups of fighters, he successfully set traps for the Germans. He knew the secret of communicating with people and had a tremendous ability to sway crowds. Seeing Dunayev enter a village, accompanied by his men, was an exciting experience.

One Sunday in August 1942, having first prepared ambushes at the approaches to the village in case any Germans might appear, Dunayev appeared in broad daylight in a church full of worshippers. He stepped up to the altar and delivered a powerful emotional speech in the style and spirit of the peasants. The entire village came pouring into the church, and the prayer meeting turned into a stormy anti-German demonstration. Accounts of this incident passed by word of mouth from one village to another, and Dunayev the partisan became a legend.

At a meeting with the Jewish partisans, Dunayev praised us for our ability and pointed out the numerous opportunities to strike against the Germans. With scorn for German technology, he convinced his men that the ordinary Russian, using his gun quickly and intelligently, would be capable of breaking the necks of the Germans. He was a person molded in the finest tradition of Russian partisans, believing that individuals were indeed capable of bringing about redemption.

Each day we trained and awaited orders for new actions. The partisan group continued to grow.

One day a Russian woman who wanted to join with the partisans was brought to headquarters. After some questioning, she was placed with the Jewish unit. She was in her twenties, beautiful, and seemingly well educated. Her name was Marusya. She said that before the war she had served in the army as a military technician. She had fled from Minsk and succeeded in reaching the partisan region during the invasion.

In the forest, she wore a military shirt and looked like an officer of the Red Army. She was especially friendly with the Jews.

Marusya was sent by headquarters to Minsk where she claimed she had connections to obtain arms. She returned to the forest with a machine gun with a bent barrel. This aroused suspicion. How could she carry a machine gun such a distance? How is it she did not notice that the barrel was bent? Wasn't she a military technician? She was sent out a second time to look for more weapons. Disguised as police, a number of partisans from another unit followed her. At the edge of the forest, the "police" arrested and questioned her. Pretending to be suspicious, the partisans accused her of spying and slapped her to convince her that they meant business.

Marusya, realizing that the situation was desperate, removed from the corner of her garment a document sewn into the hem. It identified her as an agent of the Gestapo. Maintaining their masquerade as police, the partisans ordered her to return to the forest to fulfill her mission. When she returned to staff headquarters, her face showed the signs of the beating. She broke into tears and cried that the police had caught her and beat her. That night she was interrogated, and her screams echoed throughout the camp, then there was silence, and she talked. She confessed to her role in the Gestapo. Her mission to Minsk had enabled her to inform her superiors of the strength of the partisans, both in men and weapons, and of the camp location. The following day she was brought to the Jewish unit as a prisoner. As she passed, the men spat in her face.

I remember the day she first came to the forest. I had accompanied her to headquarters. While on the way, we passed a group of Dunayev's men saying farewell to their comrades. The group had been given the difficult task of making its way to the front on foot to fulfill an important mission. There was much embracing and well wishing. As I regarded this moving

Letter by Cholawski to the Jews of Stolptzi.

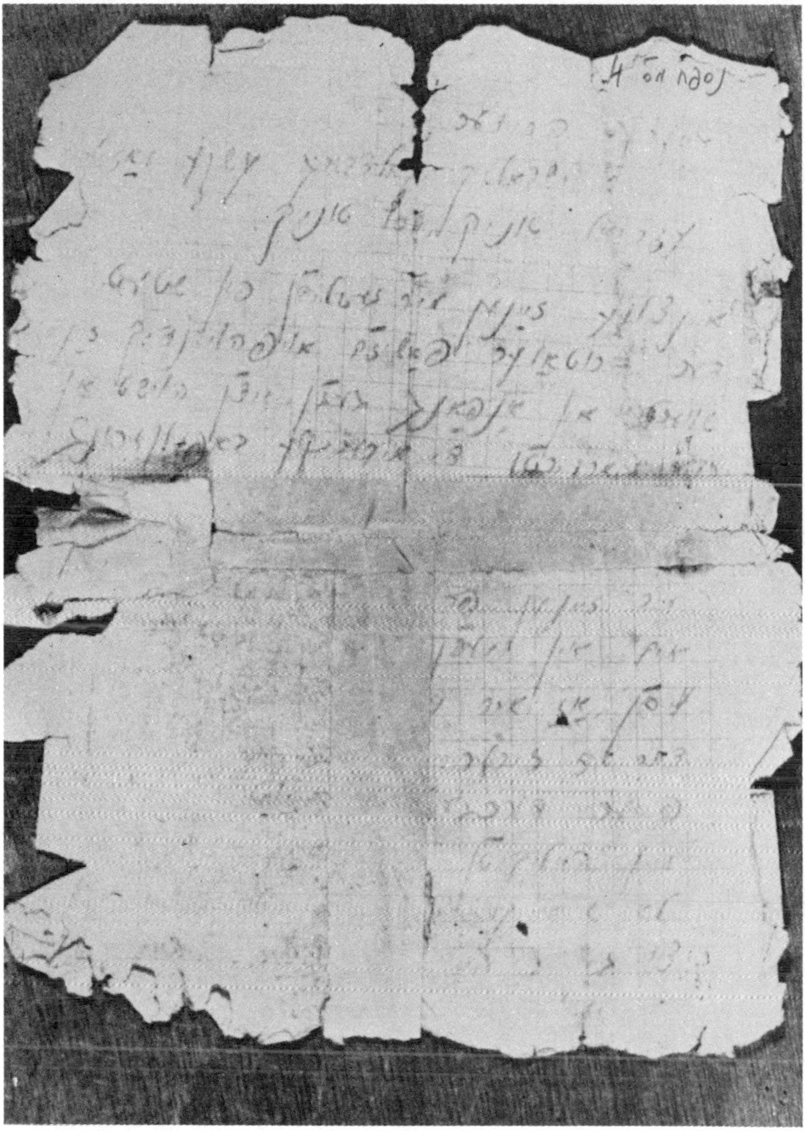

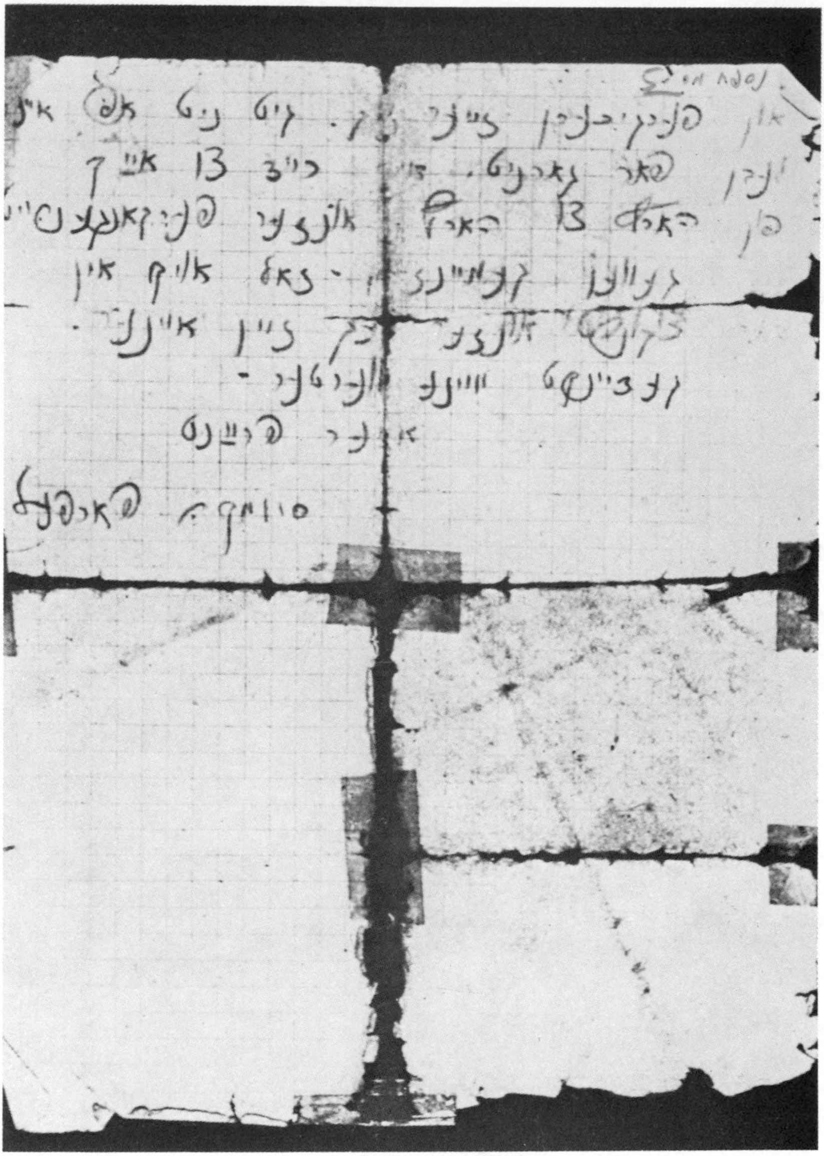

[illegible]
אין פֿערגעבן מיינע נאָך. קיט ניט אָפּ אין
ייִדן פֿאַר געהרגעט. די כ״ג צו אייך
פֿון האַלט צו האַרץ אונזער פֿאַרזאַמלונג[illegible]
געווען געמיינט. זאָל אויך אין
[illegible] אונזער נאָך זיין איינער.
[illegible] [illegible] [illegible]
אייער פֿריינט

סיומקע פֿאַרפֿעל

Letter by Siomka Farfel to Stolptzi.

Before the Liberation (1944): Right to left: Kantorowicz, Shalom Cholawski, Simcha (Sevek) Rozen.

After the Liberation and emerging from the forest: Shalom Cholawski and Hedva Lahovitzka (Eichenwald).

JEDNODNIÓWKA CENA 5 ZŁ

NASZA WALKA

ORGAN ZW. ŻYD. ZDEMOBILIZOWANYCH ŻOŁNIERZY I PARTYZANTÓW W POLSCE

ŁÓDŹ–KRAKÓW, DNIA 1 MARCA 1946

Odezwa
Bracia żołnierze żydowscy!

Przez sześć lat walczyliśmy na polach bitew Europy, w szeregach pełnej chwały Armii Czerwonej, w jednostkach odrodzonego Wojska Polskiego. Pod **Kutnem** i **Modlinem,** pod **Mławą** i w **Warszawie** we wrześniu 1939 r., pod **Stalingradem** i **Lenino** — a potem w potężnym natarciu na wszystkich frontach — walczyliśmy, pókiśmy nie zagnali wroga aż do Berlina i tam go nie zdusili.

Dzisiaj wracamy do domów jako zwycięzcy, którzy uratowali honor narodu, a stracili **wszystko.** Nasze domy leżą w gruzach. Nasi ojcowie i matki zginęli w krematoriach **Treblinki** i **Bełżca.**

Stoimy na ruinach życia żydowskiego, naszego własnego życia, osieroceni i osamotnieni.

Szesnaście tysięcy Żydów walczyło w szeregach Wojska Polskiego. Tysiące spośród nich już dzisiaj zedmobilizowano. Tysiące opuści armię polską jutro. Czy każdy z nich ma iść w swoją stronę? Czy wspólna walka ma pozostać tylko wspomnieniem? Czy nie czeka nas wspólne jutro, wspólna droga życia, wspólna przyszłość?

Czy żydowska siła zbrojna, która jeszcze wczoraj dokonywała czynów bohaterskich, ma dzisiaj, w nowej rzeczywistości, rozpadać się na tysiące odosobnionych, złamanych jednostek? Jednoczy nas walka wczorajsza, ból dzisiejszy, wiara w jutro. Zjednoczmy się!

Zjednoczmy się w niesieniu pomocy żołnierzowi żydowskiemu — naszemu bratu; w stworzeniu dlań możliwości życia i pracy, by przywrócić mu godność ludzką i siły twórcze; w zrównaniu go z całą walczącą i pracującą demokracją polską!

Zjednoczmy się, żeby przezwyciężyć trudności dnia dzisiejszego. A czeka nas walka. Walka, którą prowadzi cały naród żydowski — o swoje prawa do życia narodowego we własnym kraju.

Armie sprzymierzone zdławiły bestię hitlerowską, ale jej trucizna jeszcze działa. Nadszedł oczekiwany pokój — ale naród żydowski jest jeszcze daleki od pokoju. Wędrują drogami Europy dziesiątki tysięcy bezdomnych Żydów, przed którymi okrutna dłoń zamknęła drogę do Erec Izrael — do kraju naszych nadziei. Stańmy za nimi ławą; to jest nasza walka!

Rzućmy na szalę w tej krytycznej godzinie nasze ważkie słowo bojowca.

Razem!

"קול קורא"
לחיילים היהודיים בצבא הפולני להשתלב במאבקו של העם היהודי על זכות
קיומו ועצמאותו הלאומית בארץ ישראל
חובר ע"י יצחק צוקרמן ושלום חולבסקי

Call to Jewish soldiers in the Polish Army to take part in the struggle of the Jewish People for national independence in Eretz Israel, composed by Yitzhak Zuckerman and Shalom Cholawski, Lodz, March 1946.

At the "Pechach" House in Lodz. In the front row (right to left) Meir (Givat Hashlosha), Nathan Blizovsky, Arieh Shtundzeiger, Shmerke Kacherginsky, Zivia Lubetkin, Yitzhak Zuckerman, Shalom Cholawski.

scene, I happened to glance at Marusya. I was surprised to find her face immobile and expressionless. That she seemed unaffected then had made me wonder.

Now, as she sat tied and under guard, it was clear that she had played her role badly. That day there was a parade of the entire unit. Shestopavlov, substituting for the brigade commander, read the charges to her as she stood alone in the middle of the field. He then shot Marusya in the head with his revolver.

A general partisan command was set up in the vicinity of Moscow, and demolition experts, officers, and soldiers gathered there to undergo training, review partisan activities, and receive arms and further instructions. News was broadcast from a radio located beside a tree near the political commissar's office. This small magic box was regarded with reverence. It was like a sacred tabernacle. We were eight hundred kilometers behind enemy lines, and the radio was our only connection to the outside world. Our expectations were great, but the announcements were always brief and disappointing. It was now fifteen months since the invasion, and we waited impatiently for the news of the final death blow against the German army. Each report told of little change—a company of the enemy destroyed in the Caucasus region; two enemy tanks hit.

From the rest of the fronts we heard nothing, but we had a feeling that the Red Army was gathering strength for a massive offensive.

The German invasion had followed a period of intense planning and deception. Even if they did not believe they could conquer all of Russia, they felt they would be able to increase their control by dealing one swift blow, thereby gaining command of the vast industries of Moscow and Leningrad as well as the agricultural regions of the Ukraine and the petroleum resources of the Caucasus.

The Germans intended to encircle Moscow from the south, surrounding and cutting off the large forces of the Red Army, which was fighting nearby. They mistakenly thought they would be able to accomplish all this with one crushing attack. True, during the first four days of the war, they succeeded in encirculing four complete Russian units, and within twenty five days they had advanced about two thirds of the way between Warsaw and Moscow. Yet all this proved to be inadequate in their quest for victory. The Germans did not take into account the tremendous psychological reserves of the Russians. They soon had to confess that the Russian soldier was scornful of death.

The Red Army gathered all its strength to push back the attack—to establish a line of defense and to strike back against the enemy from the front and rear. On July 3, 1941, Stalin called upon the people to set up a partisan movement in the manner of the peasant bands that fought against Napoleon's *Grande Armée*. It was doubtful that the Russians had made any preparations for this kind of warfare. However, luckily for them and to the misfortune of the Germans, winter that year came earlier than usual, and the German offensive was arrested in December 1941 near Moscow. To disguise their failure, the Germans announced that the war in the East would depend, from now on, on the conditions of the Russian winter. The Red Army, despite its tremendous losses, was not annihilated, and Moscow was not taken. The road to Archangelsk was not cut off; Leningrad was safe.

The halting of the German march toward Moscow gave the Red Army an opportunity to regroup, and the conquered area became a hindrance to the Germans. The major part of the German transport, which depended on wheels rather than caterpillar treads, was caught in mire and along demolished roads. This strategic weakness of the Germans aided the growth of the partisan movement.

At the same time, German retaliations against local populations for their allegiance to the partisans drove more and more villagers to enlist in the fighting units. As the slaughter of peasants by the Germans increased, so did the counterflow into the forest. The Germans would send out bands of murderers disguised as partisans to plunder and murder. When these acts of deceit were disclosed, the sympathy and aid of the population for the partisans grew twofold. Gradually, the forest began to terrify the German soldier.

The Jewish unit relocated to the Staritza forest, easily accustoming itself to the new habitat. A number of Belorussians from the villages and some prisoners of war joined our company. Soon the number of Jews reached fifty or sixty and there were fifteen or twenty Belorussians. The Belorussians and Russians did not feel at home with us. For some of them, it was all too strange and unpleasant to be soldiers in a Jewish unit, and in some it was possible to distinguish, beneath a cordial exterior, a well of hate. Many of the Jewish fighers felt that in time this hate would reveal itself, but we had to be careful not to provoke it. Our work was much too important to let anything interfere.

Despite these feelings, most of the men turned to each other, acquaintances growing into friendships. *Zapadniks* "westerners" became friendly with *Wostochniks* "easterners." Lively conversation, the sound of laughter, and even singing was heard in the camp, especially during the evening campfires. Songs, like the fires, were the faithful companions of the fighters in the forest. Partisan songs were special.

At twilight during the early days of the golden Belorussian autumn, I used to walk through the forest on my way to the brigade staff headquarters to receive instructions. The excitement of the color in the wild growth of the trees restored my tired spirit. I thought my heart had closed to such feelings. As

I left the staff tent, the last lights of the dying day would be trembling among the boughs of the trees. Once, upon starting back for the Jewish camp, I heard the pleasant voice of a young girl. She was singing a new partisan song, which told of the partisans' longing for their distant homeland, of the passionate farewell to wife and family, of battles, of hopes for happy days, of a woman's tear that purifies a solitary letter.

Listen, O companies, to the song of the front:
Sure direction, steadfast heart.
To tempests of fire the homeland has sent
The best of her might for battle equipped.
In farewell, the son, mother-kissed.
A husband's good-bye, a wife embraced.
Long hours she at the station waited,
Her dear one imaged in his leaving.
On the way before the storm
There is a letter near his heart—
Better to die in battle than the shame of captivity,
Better a bullet than the enemy's mercy.
A bomb will explode, the earth will shake,
But to tremble before the gun is shameful.
The postman passes, a letter he brings,
And the writing the whole family recognizes.
Oh, tell the people if anyone will ask
That the homeland did not send him in vain.
Oh, what a meeting there will be at the station
On Victory Day, when the war is over,
And the mother kisses the letter,
The wife holds it close to her breast.

What is likely to be in the heart of a person as he hears this song, when one is an orphan, alone in the world? I was transfixed with feelings of overwhelming sadness and anger. A few days later the song was heard echoing throughout the camp. People sang it devoutly as if were a prayer of consolation. It became the first partisan song of the forest. Its strength and compassion stood us in good stead during all our days in the forest.

We were a disciplined group, but our way of life and our daily personal relationships were fashioned by the fighters' own spirit. The food was ample despite conditions in the forest and what we had grown used to in the ghetto. Bread was unlimited, and there were even enough meat and potatoes for all. Food was divided according to the unit, and with little exception, there was an equal portion for everyone, for the soldier as well as the officer, for the veteran as well as the newcomer. Provisions for the sick were excellent.

Kapusta's unit grew to well over one hundred men. The Russian commanders of the companies were Bazrokov and Byalousov. The platoon commanders were Simcha Rozen, Mikanovsky, Shmuckler, and I. Berkowitz was the chief of staff. The deputy commander for the commissary was Michael Fish. Weiner, a party man, was political commissar. Section commanders were both Jews and Russians. In the reconnaissance platoon were Mishke Neimark and Hanan. My platoon consisted, for the most part, of young people, and they were armed. Gilchik's efforts were successful in equipping the new men with weapons. The attitude of the brigade command to the Jewish unit was not always positive, but our security lay with Kapusta, who was openly fond of the men in our unit. He encouraged and assisted our development.

The partisan principles, by now, were well defined, and taught to every new member:

The tree and the darkness were our most faithful allies.
The winter was our friend, with its short day and long night.
Our main strength was in surprise and in the enemy's illusion that they were in pursuit of us.

Groups of Jewish partisans, one after another, began to undertake general reconnaissance missions to continue the search for arms. We soon learned, however, that a much more powerful weapon than arms in partisan warfare was the effect rumored strength created. A necessary precondition to feeding these rumors was to establish a rapport with the population. We worked at creating the illusion of great power. We kindled stories of force and victories. These, in turn, sparked the imaginations of the peasants who exaggerated and distorted them in the retelling.

Out of cleverly devised actions came tales of great triumphs. A group of us would surround a hostile village at night and drag a cart about the town at reckless speed creating much noise and fear. The next day, the village would speak of the three hundred partisans who had passed through the village on their way to the German command station. Once, while within hearing distance of some peasants, I ordered my men to place a machine gun at one end of the village and a second at the other end and to position the mortar on the hill opposite. In fact, we did not even have a gun for every man, but soon we heard the story that a partisan force equipped with machine guns, mortars, and artillery was preparing for a large attack. These stories fortified the loyalty of our friends, turned the doubtful in our direction, and frightened and deterred hostile elements from moving about easily in the area.

Little by little, the Jewish partisans began to learn the terrain and to become skilled at moving through the villages both at night and during the day. We acquired a nose for smelling out ambushes, but not without paying dearly for the lesson.

In the first weeks of our existence, a group of us had gone out in the direction of Mogilan to scout for food. On the way, we were surprised by a heavy barrage of German gunfire. I saw Plotek fall. A refugee from Warsaw who had

111

escaped from the Nesvizh ghetto, Plotek had just recently had the good fortune to acquire his own gun. He was the first casualty of the Jewish unit.

Despite such losses, we intensified our operations. In the fall, I commanded a squad to the Lakhovitz region. In the group was Yakov Geller, a merchant from the village of Kletsk in the Lakhovitz region who was well acquainted with the roads and the peasants. Several non-Jewish partisans joined the group. The first night we succeeded in covering a great distance and penetrating the Nesvizh region. We attacked a German dairy, damaged its equipment, and gathered into our carts everything that seemed worthwhile. As night came to an end, we made our way to a temporary base situated in a small woods in the same region.

In the late afternoon of the following day, we reached Lakhovitz, and by nightfall, we arrived at the village of Zubelevitz, three kilometers away. We left the carts at the approach to the village and held secret meetings with our contacts in Zubelevitz. We learned that there were several Germans there. We began to survey the houses under suspicion and discovered that there was a German in one of them. Surrounding the place at dark, I broke into the house with several of my men. The light from the large room was quickly extinguished, but not before we spotted the German running from the room. As I shouted, the German, who was tall and about thirty years old, froze and raised his hands above his head. We took his revolver, his rifle, and all his personal belongings. Our interchange was brief. We had caught him three kilometers from his garrison, and he had been sitting complacently in the house as if it were his own. He began to beg for his life. He showed us the picture of his wife and children. We were not insensitive to this, but we knew the dangers of the road and the impossibility of transporting him back to camp. We shot him on the spot.

There we stood, our eyes sparkling, our heads pounding

with overwhelming emotion. Our first German! German blood by the hands of Jewish partisans! We ran from the house and into the arms of the forest, which embraced and sheltered us as if we had entered the doorway of our home.

From time to time a solitary Jewish refugee would appear after roaming for months along roads and hiding in forests. As far as we knew, in the cities and towns of the whole region, there were no Jews left except at the Sverzhna camp and in Stolptzi.

We were sure that when these Jews heard of the existence of our unit from a Jewish source, they would not delay a moment in joining the fight. In September 1942, Siomka Farfel and I met with Political Commissar Weiner to discuss the matter of getting Jews out of Stolptzi and Sverzhna. We wanted to notify these Jews of our activities; they must know that Jews were killing Germans. As a party man, Weiner had closer contact with those in command at headquarters. As a Jew, he was always eager to help his fellow Jews. We told Weiner that freeing Jews from the ghetto was our primary mission. He agreed, but raised the problem of convincing the command. We decided at this meeting to establish contact with the Jews of Stolptzi on our own by dispatching letters to the youth there. Siomka had many acquaintances within the youth movement from past regional meetings and from the summer camps of *Hashomer Hatzair*. It was assumed that the Stolptzi people would subsequently get in touch with those in Sverzhna some four kilometers away. Siomka Farfel and I wrote letters. Mine went as follows:

Dear Brethren!
Yisrael Goldberg, Ozer Mazeh, Azriel Tunik, Yosef Tunik!
From all the cities and towns, just a few of us have remained. Murderous Fascism has raised its bloody sword against the Jews . . . [You have] to be the pioneers for the youth. Organize yourselves into groups. Each one of you

113

has a double mission: Revenge and Victory. Don't surrender your lives as readily as those who have fallen before you. I urge you to follow the word I will show you—that of Combat and Honor!

Fascism is weakening, and we shall overcome it. The partisan movement is a tremendous force that is growing stronger every day. You are isolated and do not know of this. Don't delay (lest) it be too late. Don't let your spirits fall. Lift your heads!

The USSR is hitting the enemy from the front. We, the partisan movement, are attacking from behind. The enemy will be beaten to the very last man. It is your duty to be among the Fighters. Be cautious, but prepare yourselves. It is the only way!

Remember,
Shalom Cholawski

P.S. Circulate this letter among our faithful friends, if they be alive: Sergovitz, and Novodvorski, Zhukovska, the teacher, and Yosselevitz, the father of Avner Aminadav and Chemda, and all our other comrades.

As for arms, gather every kind of weapon possible: grenades, guns, revolvers, bullets—each will be most valuable. Head in the direction of Kopyl. That is where we are.

Siomka Farfel's letter followed:

I just want to add a few words to what Shalom has written. Time is your enemy. Organize yourselves while it is still feasible. Your young lives are precious. Let them not be destroyed. At all cost collect weapons. Time is short. Prepare to join in the partisan life. We can no longer listen to what our elders say. We must fight. I speak from experience. Nothing will be gained by our deaths in the ghetto.

Fascism is collapsing. It is casting its last shadow on the battlefield; come hasten its defeat. Victory is on our side! Fight for your lives!

I am speaking to you from the heart.

We had a common past—may our future be one.

Remember my words,
Your friend,
Siomka Farfel

The letters were smuggled into the Stolptzi ghetto by a courier.

Before long the camp received news of the arrival of a group of Jews from Stolptzi. They were brought in by Gilchik. Our Jewish family was growing!

The group consisted of young men and women: Yosef Harkavi, Axelrod, Shmuel-Lev Oginski, Shlamek, Azriel and Hava Tunik, Moishele Weinstein, Moishele Esterkin, Kuba Altman, Ozer Mazeh, Eliyahu Ingelman, Zilla, Lazar Zaretski, Eliezer Melamed, Yulik Pintchevski, Hirsch Possessorski, Bernstein, and Reich. They had left the ghetto in two groups. At our camp the Harkavi group was reunited with the Possessorski group.

The Harkavi group was comprised mainly of members from *Hashomer Hatzair* and *Betar*. Most had been educated in the *Tarbut* Hebrew School and the youth movement. After losing his family to the Germans, Yosef Harkavi devoted himself entirely to the organization of the underground. Harkavi, Azriel Tunik, and Moshe Zartski, members of the local leadership of *Hashomer Hatzair,* were the living spirit of the Stolptzi underground. They had smuggled a radio into the ghetto and planned the bombing of the only train in town. A Belorussian, however, informed on them. The liaison man, a Jewish engineer, was arrested, and the plan was not executed. Despite setbacks, the will to succeed pushed them to devise new plans.

On an early autumn night in 1942, Harkavi and Oginski assembled seventeen young Jews. They had seven guns in their possession and several hand grenades. They stole out of the ghetto by cutting through the barbed wire, and set out in the direction of Kopyl. Harkavi told their story:

"The great forests and the open fields ouside the ghetto fence were like another world, spacious and welcoming and green. We were anxious to learn what had happened to other Jews. It was not only impossible to learn the news of the large

115

and more distant cities, but we could receive no information on what had occurred in the adjacent areas.

"In Stolptzi during the first two days after their arrival, the Germans did not bother the Jews at all. It almost seemed as if they were ignoring our presence. Some of us went so far as to believe that the refugees from western Poland had exaggerated the stories of evil concerning the advancing German troops. On the third day, new army units passed through the town. The soldiers behaved ruthlessly toward the Jews, exploding grenades in houses and indiscriminantly plundering. Then the city was bombed. The Jews abandoned their homes and fled to the fields. Death followed some there. After the shelling the remaining Jews returned to the town. The center of the village was gutted, and most of the homes destroyed. Several families crowded into one house. The Christians were delighted with our misfortune and refused to shelter us.

"Then came the decrees: 'A Jew passing a German must greet him and remove his hat six steps in front of him and five steps behind him.' We were given the 'privilege' of walking in public, but only in the middle of the road. Since the Jews had to walk in the middle of the road, the cows were herded to and from pasture on the pavement. The Christians found themselves walking together with the Jews; some, however, preferred walking with the cattle.

"The *Judenrat,* headed by Wittenberg, a refugee from Warsaw, believed that it was possible to bribe the Germans and outwit them. Frass of the *Judenrat* would tell exaggerated news reports to fortify our idealistic wishes. Catch phrases became ghetto prayers: 'Ibberleben' ('outlast'); 'zu derleben' ('to live to see'); 'Me darf hubben nor a geram yeshueh' ('All you need is a tiny bit of redemption'); 'a schlechten Deutsch, a shwereh toit; a guten Deutsch, a leichten toit' ('For a bad German, an unnatural death; for a good German, an easy death').

"Constant hunger was a gnawing beast. We fooled

ourselves to overcome the pain. Some kept a dry crust of bread in their pocket. As long as they had a piece of bread in their pockets, they had some feeling of security and a sense of having eaten their fill. When the fierce winter days and the great frost came, Jews, through chattering teeth, proclaimed, 'At least they, too, are freezing at the front.'

"The Jews were concentrated in the town slum, Yorzika. Without a tree or any greenery, this arid plot was sandwiched between two cemeteries.

"From time to time we were gathered in the cattle market for selection; the Christians looked on with delight. Then suddenly a whisper would pass along the lines: 'They're coming.' Everyone would remove his hat as a group from the Gestapo with shiny caps and polished boots would make its appearance, headed by the *Sondefuhrer* for Jewish affairs. He was a man with a cruel face, an ugly scar on one cheek, and tight lips pressed together in contempt and disgust. His twisted face was the perfect caricature of a Prussian *Junker*.

"With stick in one hand and gloves in the other, he would scrutinize us like a field marshal reviewing his troops. He demanded military discipline from the Jews, frustrated that his talent was not required at the front. The Gestapo would then pass before the rows of Jews, examining each one carefully. Whoever seemed to belong to the intelligentsia was immediately ordered out of the line. Every person with a look of protest or self-respect or whose masculinity was obvious was ordered to stand in a special line. They were always marched out of sight. The heart prophesied their end.

"When the new commandant arrived, hopes were revived. He was a Viennese professor and a senior officer. He called in the members of the *Judenrat*. He told them that he was angered by the prevalent barbarism, specifically that Jews were forced to wear badges of shame. He promised he would repeal this disgusting regulation and would ease the work burden. The men of the *Judenrat* were encouraged by this 'intelligent' officer. It took only a short time, however, for him to learn to follow in his predecessor's footsteps.

"Meanwhile, there were Jews in the ghetto who realized that the day of the German downfall would be hastened with the help of a resistence group. Several of us began to formulate a plan.

"Hirsch Possessorski worked as an interpreter at the railroad station. He smuggled arms into the ghetto by hiding the weapons in the wood transported from the railroad station; the arms were then concealed in Lazar Zaretski's cellar. Possessorski recruited young men anxious to form a group, and, in time, he became a leading person in the underground.

"Ya'akov Spiegel, born in Tomashov Mazovieck, had studied mathematics in Warsaw and was arrested for communist activity. During the Soviet period, he edited Polish programs at the Baranovichi broadcasting station. With the German invasion, he lost his wife and his two little boys. While working at a lumber yard, he was able to collect information for us from the farmers. Although we wanted him to stay in the ghetto to organize the underground, he left for the forest, together with four comrades, in the beginning of May 1942. We never heard from him again.

"Wittenberg, the chairman of the *Judenrat*, collaborated with those who organized the underground, advising us and showing us how to acquire money for arms. One of our first actions was to collect forty German uniforms so that, at the moment of the uprising, the Jews dressed in these uniforms would cause confusion and our escape would be made easier.

"The underground was organized into groups of five, but it was divided by two schools of thought. One advocated contacting the partisans and escaping to the front as soon as possible. The second wanted to prepare to fight when the Germans began their extermination. Each side defended its position vehemently; each was plagued by doubts.

"Then a sudden order came: five hundred young men from

Stolptzi were needed to work in Baranovichi and Minsk. The *Judenrat* was ordered to supply the men within a few hours. A number of the young people arose, among them Possessorski, and maintained that this was the proper time to rise in revolt. But the majority thought otherwise, and the five hundred went to Baranovichi and Minsk. The young people were left in a state of depression and confusion. 'Why didn't we act?'

"We soon heard of the liquidation of the Jews in neighboring villages. News reached the ghetto that in the village of Krishlovtchina, the Gestapo had surrounded the house of Feivel, the Jewish tailor. Feivel, still inside, set his house on fire, and when it was engulfed in flames, opened the window and leaped out onto the commandant killing the officer before he himself was killed by the other soldiers.

"The news spurred the ghetto to dig bunkers, for the only way to escape was underground. Two days after *Yom Kippur* (5703), the ghetto was surrounded by policemen and German soldiers with automatic weapons. Crowds of people pressed against the closed gate, hundreds of eyes filled with fear. A small party of Jews was removed from the ghetto by the German for an 'essential' work detail. Pits were prepared near the village of Zimna, and truckloads of Jews were directed there from the ghetto."

Harkavi paused, the flood of recent memories too much for him. Melamed continued: "Emotions were strained. I remember the horror as the multitude that had gathered pressed itself toward the closed gate, a mass of hands raised in fear. I didn't know how to act. I turned and ran to Shlomo Flay's house, where my mother was. Once inside I spotted, on a bench in the kitchen, a kneading board with some dough all prepared for baking. The dough was running over the sides, but it remained untouched. The night before the women had prepared the dough for bread. They had worked hard to get some flour, and by the early morning hours, they had already kneaded the dough. The oven was lit and the fire was burning. Red tongues of flame jumped and danced—the devil's joy. In the house the people were walking about in silence and despair.

"Shlomo Flay was pacing the length of the room, not uttering a word. His wife was wringing her hands anxiously. I went over and embraced my mother, but I couldn't say a word. 'My son, she said, 'we are condemned to death, but you are still young and you must live. Go, my son, test your fate, and may God keep you!' And with these words she gave me her scarf as a keepsake.

"It was the most difficult thing for me to do, to leave her. We embraced. My eyes filled with tears, and I broke away, running outside in the direction of the gate, pressing myself against the crowd of people, never looking back. Then the Germans began to fire into the ghetto, and everyone fled from the streets. Even the Christians who had gathered to watch the show scattered.

"I hid with one of my girl friends in a house between piles of rags and sacks of flour. Soon a mother and her three children followed us into the house. The mother hid in one corner and the children in another behind the rags. The Germans discovered the children. One of the boys began to scream, 'Mama! Mama!' As the Germans dragged the children away, one child, four years old, shouted to his brother who was crying, 'Zog nit mameh. Men vet ir oich zunemen' ('Don't say mama, they'll take her too').

"I will always hear that, especially at night: 'Zog nit mameh.' And I will always remember the sight of the mother as she watched her children being dragged away by the Germans. She was hitting her head against the wall, as if to punish herself for remaining silent, for wanting to live."

Melamed became silent, and Possessorski continued the story: "No revolt took place, but the conviction to escape to the forest was firmly established. I planned the exodus for

120

myself and any willing Jew working with me at the railroad station. At twelve o'clock noon, when the officer on duty called 'lunch', I stole into the officers' room where the Germans had left their belts. I removed five revolvers, dropping them into my trousers, which were fastened at the cuffs with clips. I then signaled to Reich, the tailor, and several other Jews to follow me. Only two responded. Angry and disappointed at the lack of response, the three of us headed for the forest, which was visible on the horizon. We passed the guard at the booth, who only looked at us suspiciously. Then we successfully slipped across a dangerous railroad bridge, crossed over an open field, and headed for the edge of the forest, the free world.

"I later found out that others had tried to escape—Melamed, Pintchevski, and Figa. Hardly had they reached the forest when the police fired a volley of shots at them. Figa was killed. The other two lost their way in the forest and barely made it back to the ghetto, armed with the intent to try again. Meanwhile, we turned eastward, hearing of Kapusta and the Jewish unit. We were delayed when my revolver, which was unlocked, went off and wounded me in the leg. After camping in one spot for a few days while I healed, we continued our search for the Jewish unit. On the way, we had an unusual meeting, which left a deep impression on us.

"One day, in our wandering, we came upon a house. It was very clean, and when we were shown in, we were unexpectedly surrounded by a pleasant atmosphere not usually found in a Belorussian home. We asked for something to drink, and the woman of the house boiled some water for tea. We were invited to supper. The man of the house, his wife, and ten-year-old son sat with us. The man was a blacksmith, and they were strict Baptists. We were impressed by their gentility. They didn't offer us something to eat in the manner that one feeds some poor unfortunate. They treated us as if we were important guests bringing pleasure and honor to their home.

121

"When we asked them if they were not afraid of us, the man replied, that he was afraid only of God. He showered us with words of encouragement, how we should not lose hope. 'Hitler will not annihilate you,' he said, 'because you are eternal and Israel is immortal. God is only punishing you for your sins and testing your faith.' When we asked him if we had sinned more than other people, he replied emphatically, 'No, your sins are less than their sins. But you are the beloved children of the Lord, His Chosen People, and, therefore, He punishes you. God chose you in order to purify the world from wickedness and to bring redemption to mankind.' He said this with such innocent simplicity and with such profound faith that we could not doubt his sincerity. When the meal was over, we went into another room. The woman busied herself getting the fire ready with little splints, and he read us passsages from a book about the mission of the Jewish people, about the suffering with which God tests His people, about the history of the Jews and their long wanderings, and about the great destiny of this people, as the leader of all peoples.

"I didn't react as deeply to the content of the words as I did to the warm, soothing voice of this man, a voice of nobility, spirit, and tender strength. When we left the house, it was already close to midnight. We made our way, in the dark and in the autumn cold, toward the great patch of forest that was to be our home. There, lying on the cold wet earth, we huddled close to each other for warmth.

"At an isolated house near the forest, we came upon Harkavi, Melamed, and others. Together we numbered over twenty. As we set out to look for the partisan camp, to our great surprise, there soon appeared gun barrels and *kubanka* fur hats with red stars—partisans! Two Russian partisans led us through Mohilna, a town devoid of Jews, to another village, Piasetchno, where the partisan command was located.

122

"The members of our group were summoned one by one to appear before the commandant. After we were interrogated, we were given an order: 'All arms are to be handed over to the Command. In the forest, you will receive other arms.'

"We were angry and confused. How could we just hand over the arms for which some gave their lives in the ghetto?—the arms which made proud men out of victims?

"Yosef Harkavi opposed the order, swearing that we would defend ourselves in battle if necesary to keep our guns. Yosef was daring and stubborn, but the rest of us asked ourselves whether it was worthwhile endangering our chances for victory and our lives after having come so far.

"We handed over the arms with a heavy heart, and in exchange we received an unsigned receipt. We were ashamed and angry. The commandant then ordered us to bring arms from the Germans; only after that would we be accepted into the unit. The ideal image of the partisan, that picture of unity, comradeship, and hope, took on an ugly look."

Gilchik soon learned of these new Jewish recruits, and accompanied by Fish, he brought them to our unit. The attitude of these exhausted Jews from Stolptzi quickly reversed again once they met Gilchik, and as they settled down for the night with their fellow Jewish partisans, they inspired us with accounts of their escapades.

The number of operations increased as our range of influence spread. In October 1942, thirty of us from the Jewish unit joined Dunayev and his men to destroy the police post at Doktorovitz, an armed garrison in partisan territory. Near the village, Dunayev gathered the fighters and explained, "This is an important operation. Be alert! You must act quickly, strike like lightning. You must fall upon the enemy like a tempest and annihilate them. Do not concern yourselves with *barachlo* ('things, clothes'). We are here for

123

one purpose only." We quickly surrounded the village and organized ourselves for battle. As we attacked, we realized that most of the police had fled minutes before. Those remaining we shot, except, for two whom we took prisoner. The police post was set on fire, and the houses of the police were bombed. In the end, our only success was in the booty we seized—clothes, food, shoes.

The partisan unit grew. Belorussians, Russians, and Ukrainians who had escaped from prison camps came to join our ranks. Zaretski, a lad of seventeen, left the forest to recruit Jews from the underground in a nearby ghetto. When he got there, he found that many objected to venturing into the forest. They forbade him to influence others and finally forced him out of the ghetto. He was captured near the barbed wire fence and executed by the Belorussian police. He was sacrificed by those whom he had tried to rescue.

The news from the front was as monotonous as a broken record: "The enemy is waiting at the gates of the Caucasus. One of their companies has been destroyed. A number of tanks have been damaged." Who knew how long this would continue? What seemed clear was that the Red Army and the invaders were destined to meet in one mighty, deciding battle. When would it be? Would the enemy cross the Volga and break through to the Urals pushing with two arms northward and southward, reaching the Caspian Sea and surrounding Moscow from the east? There was still hope that the Russians would eventually be victorious, but when? The end of the war was nowhere on the horizon.

One night, while on guard duty, I went out to check the posts. When I came to one observation post, I called to the guard. No response came. I thought he had fallen asleep. When I came within a few meters of him, he stopped me. "What's with you, Hanan?" I asked. "Did you fall asleep?"

Hanan was a young fellow from Kopyl. He was brave, responsible, one of our best scouts. "I didn't fall asleep," was his answer. "I was lost in thought." "Look," he said, putting words to his thoughts, "the end of the war is not yet in view, and perhaps this is just the beginning. A skirmish here and a raid there. What about us? Our lives are suspended in doubt each day, each moment. Just a few days ago, I was on reconnaissance with Mishke Neimark when we stepped into a German ambush. We came within inches of dying. I don't know how we ever got out alive from under that rain of fire. What about next time? How many times can miracles take place? Once, twice . . .? In the end, bullets do hit their mark. One day we will drop somewhere, alone, like a dog in a field, with no witness to mourn our passing."

Hanan's voice broke. I left quietly, hoping my face did not reveal my own fears.

With the coming of winter, we began to make preparations. The older folks, the women, and children were sheltered several kilometers from the fighting unit. Only able-bodied men remained in the camp. We began to build wooden huts and dig storage pits for potatoes, grain, and fat. Hay was gathered for the horses and cattle. All this had to be carefully camouflaged. For weeks we hoarded supplies of food into the underground store of the Staritza forests. It was a strange picture to see row after row of carts loaded with produce from the field being piled into our storage bin—so much abundance in a time of such deprivation.

In the midst of this necessary and serious work, preparations for the twenty-fifth celebration of the October Revolution began. The officers were busy training the fighters for the parade. The head of the brigade staff, Captain Reboz, supervised the activities. A platform was set up in a clearing and, next to it, room for the two brigade bands. A large quantity of whiskey was brought in, as well as rich desserts to sweeten the feast. At daybreak on the holiday, everyone excitedly dressed for the parade. The enthusiastic devotees of the October Revolution were already tipsy with joy, adding to the festive mood. The food was spread out and people began to line up to view the parade. Then, quite suddenly, without a moment's warning, from the neighboring village came a runner with the news—"Germans! Germans!" Thousands of them with tanks and artillery had entered the villages in the area. Immediately the mood of the day shifted. Without hesitation, the units of the brigade took their positions at the edge of the forest to guard the roads on either side. Wagons were quickly loaded. The command gave instructions to move the convoy to the larger forests and the marsh areas not far from the Staritza forests. Just a few kilometers from the camp, they encountered a large German force, which attacked with a heavy barrage of fire. Some of the wagons were captured; the rest raced back to the forest. Moishele Weinstein was brought to camp severely wounded.

By the afternoon the Germans had encircled the forest. Their first assault was repulsed. The enemy apparently did not want to reveal their full power, hoping to learn our strength and exact positions. Their plan, it seemed, was to initiate an all-out attack at dawn. The brigade command gave orders to prevent the enemy from entering the forest—at all costs, to hold out until nightfall. With darkness, scouting units reconnoitered the area to find a way out of the encircled forest. We were successful in holding back the Germans though there was fighting, the heaviest in Dunayev's section.

The fighters were called in from their posts with orders to move out. The unit moved slowly and with utmost care toward the narrow strip of marshland not held by the Germans, though clearly within the range of German guns. By night, the enemy sees with its ears, so it was imperative not to rustle leaves or crack the dry branches under foot. We walked on noiselessly. Lolak's mother from Kopyl fell into a brook on the way, and soon her wet skirts froze. Each of her movements made the crackling sound of branches being crushed under the weight of feet. Hers was the only noise that could be heard.

126

The unit, consisting of two companies, crossed through the no-man's land. The first company was commanded by Byalousov, the second by Gilchik. To fully protect themselves, the companies had to penetrate deeply into the region of the great forests known as the Vorovyova forest. The crossing proved hazardous for the Jewish partisans, not just because of the terrain. During the trek, which lasted five or six days, Byalousov's fanatical anti-semitic feelings emerged. Though we marched through the swamp shivering with cold and hunger, Byalousov made no effort to ease our suffering. Whatever potatoes there were went to the non-Jewish section. Search parties comprised only of non-Jews were sent out to scavenge the area to claim what they found for themselves. For the "offense" of taking a garment from a peasant's house, two Jewish fighters were stripped of their arms. As we came closer to our destination, the Lavi forest, where Kapusta's entire brigade was located, Byalousov began to cover up for his behavior. But we did not forget, and for a long time Byalousov was ostracized by the unit.

At the meeting of the brigade command, the events of the past days were summarized. It was clear that the Germans, who had come to Staritza arrogantly confident, had departed angrily. The entire brigade had successfully slipped away from the encampment, and the Germans were left to fight bravely with trees. There were fatalities, however. The Dunayev unit had organized an ambush for the Germans. Many Germans were killed and wounded, and five small tanks were hit. But in this successful raid, five partisans lost their lives, Dunayev among them. His death was a great shock. This partisan commander was admired by everyone in the brigade for his integrity, his military acumen, and most of all for his humanity.

The brigade camped in the Lavi forest. The Jewish unit, the women, and the children settled in the nearby village of Yavishtche. After that cold and hungry November, these next few weeks were a relief. We lived in the warm houses of peasants, sharing their food and resting. In the course of these weeks, solid friendships were formed. The partisans supplied the food and the peasant women added their personal touch to the cooking. The dishes had that home-cooked taste so long forgotten.

In early December, at Yavishtche, we received the greatest and most joyous piece of news—the tide of war had turned! The enemy was surrounded in Stalingrad! True, the enemy forces were not entirely crushed, for the steel ring of the Red Army had only just begun to press in toward the beaten enemy. But this was the moment we had been waiting for. The contented, at-home feeling and the encouraging news excited everyone, inspired confidence, and brought about the realization that the battle would soon be won. Upon the arrival of a group of Jews from Baranovichi our joy was unbounded. Led by Vishniya and Liess, the group numbered twelve and included the Kvass sisters and Azriel Tunik with his two sons. They brought a machine gun with them, five rifles, several hand grenades, and thousands of rounds of ammunition. These Jews were welcomed warmly and placed in the houses where the Jewish fighters were lodged.

One late December day there came a sudden alarm. Many well armed enemy units had attacked the brigade just beyond the village of Lavi. The brigade jumped into readiness. The finest fighting units began to mobilize to confront the enemy that had dared to break through the forest.

At dawn that day, the enemy forces had moved toward Lavi. They wanted to attack the partisan brigade by surprise. Waiting for them on a hill that dominated the cemetery near the crossroads was a partisan force numbering eighteen men. An effective and concentrated volley of fire by the partisans greeted the large forces of overconfident Germans. Their advance was stopped. They regrouped and returned fire. Seventeen partisans fell in this battle, and only one succeeded in breaking through the enemy lines. The battle gave sufficient time for the entire brigade to organize itself, to mobilize, and to lay in ambush against the enemy. As the German force again began its advance, it was surprised by fire from the brigade. With its advantage lost, the enemy sustained heavy losses and quickly retreated. The battle of Lavi was a victory for the partisans, and one of the most illustrious achievements of the brigade. The seventeen men who died defending their post against impossible odds were responsible for the victory. A song was composed in their memory. "The Battle of Lavi" echoed throughout the partisan camp and the forests of Belorussia:

Morning, morning and dawn is still not up.
Groups of the enemy creeping, encircling
In ambush, the fighters are not sleeping.
Quickly the camp aroused to battle.
Gunfire split the air.
A hurried command: To arms!
And the companies of men revenging a people
Encircled the enemy with a ring of fire.

Toward the winter the brigade decided to move to Orliki, a region of great forests at the northern end of Polesye. It was too dangerous to stay in the small forests. The road was long, and the Brigade was forced to cross the Moscow-Warsaw road. Sleigh tracks and foot prints in the winter snow revealed the course of the partisans, but we arrived at the destination without trouble. The new forest welcomed us with a freezing, stinging snow.

Polesye, the land of the great marshes, is shaped like a triangle. At its apex is Brisk; at its base are the waters of the Dnieper River. This broad country is veined with numerous brooks and streams that gather and channel through the upper heights of central Belorussia in the north and the

Wohlinia heights in the south. Railroads, the vital transport arteries of the German army, cut through Polesye from Brisk and Leningrad, and they converged on Moscow from Pinsk through Baranovichi, Minsk, and Smolensk.

The population of Polesye was sparse. Those who did not breed small herds of cattle or till the soil cut and sold timber. For most of the year, the small villages were cut off from each other and from the neighboring towns by the marshes. Only in winter could peasants of Polesye venture out across the snow-covered expanses on sleighs to the regional town. They went with their few head of cattle or with sleighs of timber to exchange for salt, kerosene, matches, salted fish, and cheap clothes for their families. These excursions, undertaken two or three times each winter, were the only contacts the villagers had with the outside world.

Polesye was ideal for partisan warfare. Partisan battles had taken place there during the Russian Civil War. The first partisan units of World War II had been organized in these regions. The most famous among them were the Linkov (Batya) and Komarov brigades, which were organized in the early spring of 1942. Partisan groups had been successful in damaging the rail lines. Despite German retaliations, most of the villages remained neutral. The Germans visited them by day, the partisans by night. In the partisan struggle to overcome the German units, Polesye came to be known as "Little Earth of Mother Russia." At the end of the year we arrived—The Kapusta Brigade.

The brigade set up camp at Orliki. Each unit was spaced several kilometers from the next, surrounding the brigade's staff headquarters. After a day's rest, the fighters began to build temporary dwellings, not light shelters as before, but wooden huts made from tree trunks. On scouting expeditions, some partisans became acquainted with the local villagers and brought back materials to aid in the construction—pipes and pieces of glass and tin. A sackcloth curtain usually served as the door. Those with expensive taste chose the wood of white birches, and the insides of these dwellings would seem to have been coated with a shiny white veneer. The furnishings of our dwelling included a small table and a wooden bed padded with straw and covered with a blanket. A few pieces of wood served as the floor. Suddenly this makeshift structure became home. When the fighter returned from a military operation or from long hours on guard duty, the *zhemlanka* offered light, warmth, and comfort.

Stringent defense measures were set up to protect the brigade. Each unit set up a watch around its base and the brigade set up a ring of defense posts eight to twelve kilometers from the staff center. They were spaced along the roads and rivers leading to the forest. In case of an ambush against a unit, that unit was to open fire, thereby giving sufficient time for the brigade to organize. Every unit was equipped with at least one machine gun. Fires were forbidden in order to avoid attracting the enemy. Reconnaissance guards on horseback made daily trips to each defense unit to maintain contact and to bring any news that might have been obtained from helpful peasants. Guard duty was divided into shifts—four hours on, eight hours off. Afraid of freezing to death, we slept only four hours of our time off. The rest of the time was disconcerting, for it left us free to think and reflect.

Partisan life in the forests of Orliki was almost appealing: affairs were organized, our shelters were warm and the food was good. Three times a day we had bread, and sometimes we had meat chunks fried in fat or cereal cooked with fat. The fat shielded us from the cold and illness. There was always tea and fried potato *latkes* ("pancakes").

131

Maintaining personal cleanliness was a constant problem for partisans, but staying in one place offered a solution. We waved our clothes through the stoves' hot air, paying particular attention to the seams; this would burn out the lice.

Liquor was an important part of our existence. It made one forget temporarily. It inspired and uplifted. Sometimes it killed. Drinking during a mission, common among the non-Jewish partisans, caused many accidents and even fatalities.

Fear and loneliness prompted relationships. A woman in the camp did not need to seek protection from a man. Everyone sought companionship and compassion in another who was experiencing the same desperation. Closeness was a mutual need. Life stirred within each *zhemlanka* under the cover of winter's snow and silence.

I shared my hut with Farfel, Rozen, Nissenbaum and Meierovitz. In the evenings, we turned our home into a Jewish club. German war candles were lit. Someone would fry *latkes* and boil water for tea. A long lost feeling of *Yiddishkeit* would float back to us, stroking our memories. We sat together, all brethen welcome, and shared stories of our Jewish community back home. We would speak of the *shtetl* as if it were still thriving and bustling, filled with the noises and the business of daily life, as if we were on holiday and unexpectedly came across acquaintances from the same city. Sometimes, Siomka Farfel would read poems to us in Yiddish, poems which he wrote in the forest. They were written with a kind of fervent passion and captured the true spirit of the fighter. Kenigstein, a tenor, would sing folk songs and tunes from the Jewish theater. Rozen of Warsaw would recite the songs of Vertinski, a well-known Russian singer of the early 1900s:

O don't cry, my beautiful one
Don't cry, my darling, my darling one
Our lives will still more beautiful be
And spring will bloom profusely.

One of the songs we all sang was "Dark Night," which expressed the longing of the fighter for his wife and child:

Dark Night . . .
Bullets whistle through the field
The winds moan through the wires
The stars blink with sadness
Dark Night . . .
My Beloved one sits
By the cradle of a babe
She wipes a tear
How I adore
The depth of your lovely eyes
How much I desire
To fix my lips upon them
Dark Night . . .
Between you and me, my darling,
There are black fields of terror
They are between you and me.

The power of these melodies transported us to a mythical world where existed none of our present fears. But reality, as is its nature, always broke through, shattering our reverie.

In the first days after our arrival in the Orliki forests, four of our members fell in an ambush. A "patriotic" peasant detected the existence of one of our units and informed the Smitzchiv police. We were encircled by a large force of Belorussian police and Germans. The partisans fought until their ammunition gave out and then they blew themselves up with grenades. Those who fell were Loptitski of Nesvizh, Azriel Tunik of Stolptzi, a third Jew, and a Russian. They were given a military funeral near the crossroads at the entrance to the Orliki forests.

One of our biggest operations was the attack on the Hantzevitz-Deniskovitz railroad line, where, according to underground information, timber was being transported under German supervision. Two groups of partisans, one from the Zhukov unit, the other from Dunayev's, were sent to intercept the cargo and impede rail service. I was among the group of Jewish fighters; in command was Commissar Martinov. We traveled for two days, secured a position near the tracks, and waited for the train. A peasant woman who passed not far from our place of ambush informed the Germans in Deniskovitz of our position. The Germans, equipped with the knowledge of our whereabouts, intended to launch a surprise attack from several directions. A large backup force was placed on the train.

But we were suspicious of the curious peasant woman, so we moved our position closer to Deniskovitz on a hill where the railroad cut through its middle forming a tunnel. We mined the tracks and took up positions on either side. After several hours of silent expectation, the train arrived. From the distance we could see that the first cars were open and full of Germans. As the train drew closer, I spotted among the Germans in the first car the peasant woman, who was acting as their guide. As the train began to pass through the tunnel the mines were set off. The tremendous explosion shattered the train. We fired at the Germans and threw grenades. The Germans, dazed by the roar and surprise, jumped from the train and hurled themselves against the wall of the tunnel. We excitedly anticipated victory, and pressed toward the enemy. The men in Dunayev's unit, however, though heavily armed with machine guns, hurriedly retreated some distance into the forest. The Germans nearer to us suffered heavy casualties from our fire, but those who were pressed against the wall near where Dunayev's men were to have been positioned recovered from their shock and began to counterattack. Without Dunayev's men, we could not fend off the attack. We were forced to retreat. Forty-five Germans were killed or injured. We suffered no losses, but the attack was unsuccessful. Dunayev's men had enabled most of the Germans to escape. The cowardly action of our fellow partisans confused us. Strong feelings of anti-Semitism had surfaced again.

When we returned to base, Brigade Commander Kapusta praised us, but made no mention of the curious action of Dunayev's unit. Some time later Kapusta flew to Moscow to report on the brigade's activities, and the atmosphere became more oppressive for the Jewish unit. We began to feel very uneasy and uncertain.

Meanwhile, a number of Jews straggled into our unit. Shalom Katchanovski reached us after the other members of his group, seven in number, hd been killed on the way due to a peasant informer. Katchanovski was a member of the movement and the Baranovichi underground. Together with Moma Kopelovitz, another member of the movement, Shalom organized youth groups and succeeded in smuggling arms from Feldzug B, the German arms store in the ghetto. Vishniya and two other partisans left for Baranovichi, carrying a letter from me to a contact, Mira Epstein, urging fellow Jews to join us. Vishniya returned with new recruits: Genia Mazurska, a nurse, her cousin, Gita, and Eliezer Segal. They were among the few who were saved from the Hantchevitz ghetto.

Changes took place within the unit. Captain Voloshkevitz was appointed chief of staff. He was a shrewd soldier, though taciturn and melancholy. Pepapenko was appointed head of the "Special Platoon"; Karlovitz was made commander of a company. They were sent to us by the brigade staff center. Among those who were also sent from the ranks of the Russian army were soldiers who wore their anti-Semitic badges as proudly as if they were medals. Morozov replaced Martinov as unit commissar. He was as incompetent as he was insecure. He proposed to separate the families from the partisans, moving them several kilometers from the camp.

Shestopavlov, likewise unstable and blatantly anti-Semitic,

informed us at a unit review that any illusions we might harbor concerning our surviving the war should be dispelled as "ninety five percent of us would be dead by then." Morozov carried out the first stage of his plan for family resettlement. The old Jews, women, and children were placed some distance from the unit in a small area that we called Siberia. They became known as *farshikte,* those who are exiled. The Jewish unit took it upon itself to look after these exiles, supplying food, clothing, and security.

The winter of 1942—1943, their second in Russia, weakened the Germans. Their dream of capturing Stalingrad and encircling Moscow began to fade. At the same time, the Russians slowly gathered military experience, equipment, and force. Battles around Moscow slowly turned the tide of the war. The Russian counterattack on the Stalingrad front in the winter of 1942 spurred the partisans to initiate extensive actions behind enemy lines.

The victories at Stalingrad turned the sympathies of the population toward the partisans. With the help of the villagers, our activities increased, and small police posts were wiped out. The town of Krasna-Sloboda was emptied of Germans and police. However, in the towns of Smiziva, Zaustirovitz, and Locatishi, there still remained large police stations. The station in Locatishi, especially, repeatedly intercepted our contacts.

The Jewish unit was assigned to wipe out the police station there. We set out toward the village, some sixty to seventy fighting men with Gilchik in command. It was a bitter cold day. At dusk we reached Locatishi. The largest force rushed the main road of the village, heading for the police station. My platoon spread out along the perimeter of the village ready to cut down those fleeing from the station. The crack of explosions suddenly shattered the silence. The police scattered. Some were caught; others were shot. We blew up the station and then set fire to the houses of the police and their collaborators. We marched through the village leaving behind us a wall of flames. Terrified peasants surrendered to us. We returned to the forest with the knowledge that through the strength and victory of the Jewish unit, we had gained respect from the villagers, the enemy, and the brigade.

In the middle of January 1943, I fell sick with typhoid fever. Despite my illness, I consulted with Possessorski on the fate of the Sverzhna Jews. Sverzhna was a work camp, the only place in the entire region other than Minsk where Jews still survived. We thought it likely that the Germans, in retaliation for their failures on the various fronts, would take their revenge on these Jews. News from our connections seemed to substantiate these fears. It was impossible to delay action until I had recuperated so I gave Possessorski the addresses of my contacts in Sverzhna. His mission was twofold: to set fire to the sawmill in Sverzhna and to recruit and organize the Jews for our cause.

Dressed like a peasant, Possessorski entered the camp, treating the German guard at the gate to a bottle of vodka. He had no sooner slipped into the camp, than he sought out his brother-in-law Zlotovitz and a comrade, Yoselevski, both in the underground. Possessorski entreated them to get out of the camp that day and to organize themselves immediately. Its plan for a breakout ready, the underground spread the word that the time was ripe. At a signal, the men ran quickly toward the fence. Quietly, they disappeared through a hole and out into the darkness. After some time, they heard a series of shots, but by then they were safely out of reach of any bullets. Some members of the group headed toward the Naliboki forests; the majority toward the Kopyl forests. The snow was deep, and many developed frostbite after crossing the stream that flowed near Sverzhna. Possessorski gave the group courage with the security of a destination—the partisan forest. He secured twenty sleighs, which were "donated" at gunpoint by some peasants. The group reached Yavishtche, and from there, via the Warsaw highway, they went in the direction of Orliki.

The first sight of a partisan unit by the group startled and amazed them. They thought partisans lived in caves and were bearded and unkempt like cavemen—afraid of leaving their earth pits in daylight! Suddenly, before them stood an organized, clean, armed group, almost as large as an army, and patrolling the forest in broad daylight. They were overjoyed.

On January 29, 1943, one hundred and twenty Jews from Sverzhna reached the Orliki district. Shestopavlov, the brigade commander, and the Jewish commanders went out to welcome them. The Jews were told they must hand over all their baggage, money, and jewlery in exchange for arms. They gladly complied. The veteran Jewish fighters in Orliki received the newcomers with open arms. We invited them to our "homes" and began indoctrinating, instructing, and supporting them. The Jewish unit was growing in strength. Many of the newcomers who came were youngsters, educated in the youth movement and the Hebrew school and active in the underground. Acquaintances and old friends from neighboring towns greeted one another with joyful embraces.

Having recovered from my illness, I invited Monik Yosselevski and Niomka Vilitovski, who were attached to my company, to bunk with me in my *zhemlanka*. Both had graduated from the Sverzhna school and were members of *Hashomer Hatzair*. They had known my younger brothers. My hut, which I was sharing with Farfel, Rozen, Meierovitz, and Nissenbaum, began to look like a small barracks with the addition of the new recruits.

We sat before the stove exchanging stories of imprisonment at the hands of the Germans. Monik recounted how he had been taken prisoner while trying to flee from his town when the enemy overcame the retreating Red Army. He was returned to his parents' home, where his little sister, Zippi, aged ten, gave him a yellow badge to fasten to his shirt: "It weighed heavily on my back like a millstone. The day after *Yom Kippur,* the Gestapo came and took thirty Jewish boys and girls to the town graveyard. The boys were ordered to dig their own graves. In groups of five, they were all shot and thrown in. A Belorussian policeman told us later that Doba, Niomka's seventeen-year-old sister, in defiance of imminent death and with a clenched fist, cried out to the Gestapo: 'There will arise the Jewish arm to avenge our blood. You will pay, you German murderers.' Doba's words became our pledge.

"A ghetto with five hundred people was set up in the town. In November all of us were assembled in the square. An order was issued for every Jew to hand over all gold and jewelry. All the men were ordered to work at the sawmill.

"About 130 men and boys, among them Niomka and myself, were herded in the direction of the sawmill. The moment we were some distance from the square, a blast of gunfire ripped the air. Our ears caught the groans of the wounded and dying, of parents screaming, of children crying. As we stood looking back, unable to help our families, we saw the *goyim* joyfully digging the graves for the *Zhids.* Corpses of children were rolled about the streets. That evening we were brought back to the ghetto under heavy guard. Our homes had been broken into and plundered; bodies were still lying in backyards and gardens."

The first underground circle was established by Monik, Niomka, Natan Goldstein, Yitzhak Perzovitz, and Yosef Adonielo. Plans were made for their escape. Niomka picked up the story: "The first step was to sabotage a section of the fence we were forced to put up around the camp. Nails were

139

set halfway into the boards so that we could break through easily if need be. Our next step was to acquire arms. Perzovitz traded his watch for a grenade from a *shegetz,* a school acquaintance. The grenade, our first, strengthened our hope. We fashioned similar grenades from wood as a ploy to frighten the enemy during our flight. We got hold of some guns and thirty rounds of ammunition. I was responsible for concealing the weapons. There was a family of Jewish tailors in Sverzhna by the name of Mankas. They sewed garments at the sawmill for the Germans and the Ukrainians. Gedalya, the son, established contact with a Ukrainian, Tchorni, promising to attend to his needs in return for ammunition. When he received his garments, Tchorni handed over a box of ammunition to Gedalya. Tchorni then told his friends, the Germans, about the exchange. A search was made, and the ammunition was discovered. Gedalya was arrested. He was tortured, but revealed nothing about the underground's activities. Gedalya's father, Shmuel David, knew that his son would not survive the inquisition. He rent his jacket as a sign of mourning, strung a rope, and hanged himself. The death of Gedalya and his father toughened the spirit of the underground.

"When winter came, activity in the underground intensified. And then, as if planned and right on time, Possessorski arrived dressed in a large sheepskin coat; on his head was a huge cap with ear muffs; and in his hand was a revolver. I wanted to embrace this shaggy creature. On his command we organized ourselves and jumped into action. The underground staff held its last meeting. We would break through the fence where nails had been placed. At nine o'clock that evening, a pebble would be tossed into every house, the signal to begin the escape.

"At 8:00 P.M. I sat eating dinner with my father, my sister, and my relatives, but the food stuck in my throat. No one in my family knew what was to take place. Finally I blurted out,

140

'Listen to me, my dear ones. In a few minutes, a revolt is going to take place here. We're breaking through the fence and getting away. We're going to cross the Sverzhna-Nesvizh road in the direction of the forest.' My family was speechless. I barely saw my father nod his approval. At the toss of a pebble, I ran from my house, heading for the hole in the fence. On the way, I ripped from my shirt that shameful badge.''

On February 7, 1943, I led a group of partisans, beginners and veterans, on a mission to gather food in Lochtishi. On the way we had to cross a road near Hominka, some two or three kilometers from Zaustrovitz, where another large, well-fortified police post, the strongest in the entire region, was situated. As my group approached the Hominka region, the lead rider, Shalom Katchanovski, safely passed through. Our column of sleighs followed some distance behind.

About ten meters before the woods, we were hit by a heavy barrage of enemy gun fire. Opposite the woods in the direction of Lochtishi lay a trench midway through a field. That was our only chance for cover. From there we could make our way to the forest. We dropped to our bellies and headed for that trench. The bullets buzzed over our heads, and some struck the ground richocheting into the group of wildly crawling men. Seven men fell, five Jewish partisans and two Russians. Some of us managed to reach the trench and then the forest.

After running for several hours, we came to a clearing in the wood. We headed for Moritz, one of our defense posts, forcing a peasant to take us through this dangerous region in broad daylight by sleigh. I warned the peasant that he would pay for any false move with his life. The peasant drove us through Zaustrovitz, right past the police station. The barrel of my rifle, under cover, was aimed at his head. The sleigh sped along in the morning mist. Smoke rose from the chimneys of the houses as the housewives prepared breakfast.

When we arrived in Moritz and the Jewish unit heard the news of the ambush, it immediately mobilized and set out in the direction of Hominka to collect the bodies. But Zaustrovitz and all the nearby villages were teeming with German soldiers, making it impossible to reach our dead comrades. Among the Jews that fell were some of the recent arrivals from Sverzhna: Botvinik, Burek, and Aaron Yosselevski. The fifth casualty was my friend, Siomka Farfel.

Siomka was the intellectual, the ghetto leader, the partisan fighter with ideological goals and realistic plans. He was loyal and conscientious and a true friend. He was the charmer and the poet. I cannot remember any of his poems, though the memory of the inspiration they sparked is forever etched in my heart.

The great chase began on February 10, 1943. News of large concentrations of Germans in Krasna Sloboda and neighboring villages forced the brigade to move southward to the inner regions of Polesye. It was clear that the ambush at Hominka was only the beginning of an all-out German assault against the partisans. We had to flee and regroup. The Jewish unit followed behind the other units, held back by the slow movement of the families—the aged, the youngsters, and the feeble.

A fierce frost accompanied us on this journey to the frozen marshes of Polesye. In the summer it was impossible to cross, but the cold allowed us to march along a solid bridge of ice.

On the first evening of our exodus, the partisan unit split up. We decided to encircle the advancing German force, the larger, stronger units to hit the enemy from the rear at a later time. This way the Germans would think that our smaller unit was defenseless, and they would be caught off-guard. Meanwhile, the units, continually in touch with each other, moved

142

southward, the Germans sandwiched in between. In the distance, we could see burning villages set afire by German troops.

The march continued without incident though we were frozen and exhausted. The question of food became a serious problem. All we had were scraps of bread, which had to last for days. The constant communication between the two separated units did not give us a chance to rest; we slept on the cold, wet ground. We soon discovered that spreading ashes in a clearing and placing a sheet of branches over them would serve as a warm bed. Under these conditions, we continued through the dark desolate steppes.

Added to our exhaustion, famine, and fear, we had to contend with another problem. More than one Russian would drop a remark that the root of all the troubles were the Jews, particularly the old Jews who were lagging behind and holding the group up. These remarks incited sharp exchanges of words between the veteran Jewish fighters and the Russians. Anti-Semitic venom had spread from the Germans to the Russians.

Toward the end of February, Michael Fish led a group of men some forty kilometers to secure food. In broad daylight, they advanced to the edge of the forest and, at dusk, attacked a farm. The fighters corralled four hundred cows. A small partisan force moved out in front with the cattle; a larger armed contingent remained in the rear. Fifteen kilometers from base the Germans opened pursuit. The contingent assigned to check the enemy held out for twenty minutes, but the lack of sufficient ammunition forced them to retreat. Michael Fish, in the rearguard, was killed. Sofer from Lakhovitz also fell. The remainder of the force managed to reach the brigade, and the cows were divided among the units.

We finally had meat instead of tasteless potatoes, but the price we paid in men's lives was much too severe. Michael

Fish had fled from the Nesvizh ghetto the night before the revolt. Because of his connections with the villagers in the area he had been responsible for replenishing the food supply. In our present condition, the unit trapped and food scarce, Michael felt it was his duty to find new sources of food. He died without knowing that he had succeeded.

The Germans launched a sudden attack on our base a few days after the cattle raid. The brigade immediately retreated. Zhukov, the Jewish unit, acted as rearguard. The highway was blocked by the Germans at both ends. There was no alternative but to escape to the thawing marshlands. We were forced to abandon four pieces of artillery, which we sank in the mud. The retreating column moved as quickly as possible through the icy marshes. We often sank to our chests in mud.

The older folk and the sick had courage, but they made little progress. Some were lost. Mikanovski, a Jewish convert from Warsaw who was old and sick, remained behind on the highway. It was said that he shot himself with his revolver. Brothers dragged exhausted brothers until they, too, were beyond strength. But we all made the supreme effort not to lose sight of the group. It was clear that he who lagged behind would inevitably fall into the hands of the Germans.

The melting ice cut into our flesh. The cold penetrated the bones. Our wet clothes froze, turning our clothes into confining sheets. To avoid sinking to our necks, we jumped from root to root. One slip and you drowned in the mud. One young boy could barely walk; his soles were frozen. He skipped all those hundred kilometers. We ate acorns from the oak trees and drank marsh water. At night we clung to roots of trees protruding from the marsh water, binding our bodies with ropes to avoid slipping and sinking. During this most difficult and dangerous period, nobody got sick, a cold or rheumatism. On the contrary, those who were sick got well. The powers of the body and the will to survive were overwhelming.

During the migration, however, the relationships within the unit became more sustained. It was later learned that Byalousov and Patpenko, two Russian commanders, killed two partisans from the Vasilov unit for their weapons.

When the brigade reached Marotshenka, it settled into a temporary encampment. There was so much tension that any innocuous incident was liable to initiate a clash. When a Jewish partisan took a loaf of bread from one of the peasants, Patpenko accused him of robbery and set out to punish him. Gilchik intervened and this lead to a physical fight. Patpenko, after taking a bad beating, remarked to his good friend Feshko, a known anti-Semite and a drunkard, "I almost killed this *Zhid.*"

We stopped over in Marotshenka only for a few days. The Germans had tracked us down. They were able to penetrate our defenses. A single warning shot by the guard on duty enabled us to slip back into the marshes. In the move the unit lost more elderly and sick.

We reached the dry land of Mashuki in the Kletsk region by the beginning of May. Escaping from the Germans, we crossed the sea of marshes and stood on the shore of a dry pine forest. Food restored our spirits, and we attended to our clothing and appearance. Into each wasted and weary body, after months of suffering in the Polesian marshes, new strength streamed.

Voloshkevitz of the staff command suggested that the Sverzhna men and older partisans, most of them unarmed, separate temporarily from the unit to gather weapons. Under this pretext, the brigade relieved itself of the responsibility of caring for some Jews. It was a treacherous act. The isolated Third Company turned in the direction of Lavi and Yavishtche.

Meanwhile, our group easily accustomed itself to the region. Through Segal's connections with the local peasants, we carried out a number of operations. On one of them, some men in the group were encircled by Germans as they came to a peasant's house in one of the villages. These Germans had been alerted by a peasant collaborator. The Jewish partisan Stoklitski tossed a grenade into the enemy group, allowing his comrades to escape. He was seriously wounded in the leg and was borne to Luban by Katchanovski, Yosselevski, Mazorovitz, and Natan Sobelman. From there he was flown to Moscow, but he eventually died of his wounds.

Slowly we built up our security and planned acts of sabotage. The Jewish unit secured additional guns and ammunition from the arms shipment housed at the local airport. Rozen and a group of fighting men went out on the road to Zaustrovitz to cut the telephone wires. I took a group to the Moscow-Warsaw highway to do the same. Meierovitz and a group of his men blew up a train.

Despite these small victories, internal conflict increased. On instructions from the staff command, a group of over fifty unarmed Jewish men and women were separated from the unit. Segal was put in charge of this family camp, and Weinberg was ordered to take a group of youngsters to the Kopyl region to meet up with the rest of the brigade in June. The reason given was that splitting up the group ensured safety in smaller numbers. Avraham Weinberg followed these orders reluctantly.

Weinberg and half of the group were the first to reach the Kopyl region. Soon they were joined by Possessorski's comrades and were shocked by the news that Possessorski had been murdered by Russian partisans.

It seems Possessorski and his group had set up camp near Yavishtche. The group included Eliezer Alpert, Natan Goldstein, Yitzhak Perzovitz, Natan Sobelman, Fela Weinberg, Ze'ev Klatchok, and Opperman. They had begun to acquire weapons and had made some good contacts among the peasants in the area. Anantchenko and his company from

Yarominko's brigade were roaming through the Kopyl region at the same time. They visited the Jewish group near Yavishtche. Anantchenko spied Possessorski's shiny German revolver and demanded the weapon. Possessorski answered emphatically, "A living partisan does not hand over his weapon." At that moment, Anantchenko drew his gun and threatened him, but Possessorski would not submit. Anantchenko shot him and ordered the remaining unarmed members to flee if they wanted to live. On that day, March 25, 1943, Possessorski, the proud and courageous fighter, died. He paid the full price for refusing to surrender.

When the other members of the Zhukov unit arrived at Yavishtche, they went to the scene of Possessorski's murder. They dug a grave on the road to Lavi and set up a monument in his memory. Possessorski's death more than saddened us. It infuriated everyone. Once the brigade command arrived, the Jewish fighting men did not hesitate to vent their anger before it. The Russians in the brigade staff did their best to cover up the murder. We were visited by someone from Moscow representing the Komsomol. I asked him what the reaction of the general staff would be to such a murder. He stammered and dodged the question, remarking that now was not the proper time to carry out judgment. Anantchenko was transferred to save his skin, but he was never brought forward to account for his crime.

The armed Jewish unit then received another shocking blow. Gilchik was relieved of his position as unit commander, and Baranov, a Russian officer, took his place. No explanation accompanied this order, although the official announcement came from the brigade's general staff.

The separation of the family camp and the unarmed partisan group from the fighting unit, the lack of any reaction whatsoever to the murder of Possessorski, and the removal of Gilchik from his command were signs of a deliberate policy on the part of the brigade to arouse discontent and rebellion

147

among the Jewish fighters. It was only natural that the idea to break off from the brigade began to gain support in the Jewish unit. But separation in those days was difficult, especially in an area which was populated by partisan units. Therefore it was decided to initiate a gradual break. Gilchik, Geller, and Shmuckler joined Weinberg's group in the Kopyl region. Gilchik organized and armed the group, camping near Shestopavlov's unit.

Baranov handled the delicate situation in the unit wisely. His attitude to the Jewish fighting men was one of respect and esteem. He personally made the effort to maintain a balance in the unit. Indeed, despite the change in command, the unit, numbering about 150, continued to retain its Jewish character thanks to its veterans, the Jewish founders.

We called him "Feodus." He was a child of twelve with blond hair, blue eyes, and a freckled face, a *shegetz*. He came to the forest with his mother and a gun. He was bright and friendly and was immediately liked by everyone. He was the first child in the Jewish unit and became our symbol of hope and rebirth. He automatically assumed the responsibility for his mother, eager to accept the role of a partisan and a man.

Feodus was continually in the company of the fighters. He ate with us, rested with us, sat in on our conferences, heard the latest reports. He learned how to keep his mouth shut when necessary. After a while, we presented him with a *schinel* ("military coat)" a smaller version of our own. In addition, he was equipped with a grenade and a military belt. Feodus learned how to ride a horse and soon became the assistant to the commander. Not too long after that he was equipped with an *otrezs*, a sawed-off gun.

The little partisan was attached to the unit staff commander, and he accompanied the riders of the unit to the various guard posts. At times, he would join the cavalry on reconnaissance. He spoke lively Russian, spiced with partisan slang. One knew by the confidence with which he spoke and by his firm stride that he was a true partisan. He was one of the Zhukov Jewish unit, and perhaps more than just that.

Feodus—his real name was Shraga Filler—was born in 1930 in Vishkov. In 1939, when the Germans invaded Poland, his parents moved to Krasna Sloboda. "Daddy was killed in Krasna Sloboda by the Germans," he told us. "From there, we went on to Timkovitchi in the Slutzk area. There I said *Kaddish* for my father. In Timkovitchi, I lived through three massacres. Once, we were assembled in the marketplace. The Germans ordered us to take food and provisions for a journey, but they deceived us. We were divided into two groups. One was marched out of town, the other to a back part of the village.

"Mother and I were in the latter group, but we ran down into a bunker. We were there a few hours when we suddenly heard an unfamiliar noise. It was a crowd going from Jewish house to Jewish house plundering. We heard them shouting at the top of their voices for us to open the bunker or be burned. They came nearer and nearer, but something more interesting caught their attention, and they retreated at the last moment. We remained in the bunker for five days drinking sourdough soup. On the sixth night, we left our hiding place and ran towards the fields, dragging sheep pelts, cloth, and a pair of shoes to sell to peasants for bread.

"Soon we met some armed men. I immediately sensed they were partisans. They were from the Vilshin unit. They regarded us with suspicion and told us we would need a weapon otherwise they wouldn't accept us. We decided to go to Lavi to try our luck there. On the way, mother hid, and I told passing peasants that I was alone and hungry. They gave me pancakes and pieces of cheese. One of them questioned me, 'Aren't you a little *Zhid*?'

"We met a kindly *goy,* and we told him we wanted to get to

149

the partisans. He said, 'They won't take you without a gun. Just wait, and I'll bring you a gun and some milk.' Mother was terribly scared that he would hand us over, but he returned with a gun for us. In turn, we gave him a pair of polished shoes and a velvet jacket, the last of our possessions. We then ran quickly to the forest where we met you brave partisans of Kapusta's unit.''

Kapusta and Kombrig, the brigade commander, were fond of Feodus. He was sent with a group of Russian partisans to one of the villages in the neighborhood to bring back fodder for the horses of the brigade command. On the way they came across a wounded Jewish girl from Kletsk. The partisans turned to Feodus and asked him to speak to her in Yiddish. With difficulty, he composed a few questions with the little Yiddish he could recall, and then he happily ran over to his comrades to recommend her. Thanks to Feodus, the girl was brought to our group in the forest.

Feodus always volunteered for special tasks in battles and missions. In the great chase and the march across the marshes of Polesye, he became separated from the group. He later told us that the partisan As's nine-year-old son and he trekked together to the camp. They ran into German patrols but fled with their lives. They evaded the wild beasts as well and survived on cranberries. After wandering for days, they distinguished the figures of our men. As they ran to us, we cried with joy, "Feodusik! Feodusik!"

Other children also proved to be courageous and shrewd survivors. Simmek Possessorski and his sister Henya, separated from their partisan brother Hirsch, had fled from an *Aktion* to the Jewish camp at Sverzhna where their brother-in-law, Zlotovitz, lived. The Jews in the camp saw before them two small children shocked, terrified, tears streaming from their eyes, unable to utter a word. They brought them into the camp and comforted them. With kindness and understanding, the children began to respond, and it was not long before they were inducted into the underground.

When the members had to discuss secret matters, they would gather in one of the rooms of the Sverzhna synagogue. Zlotovitz would come out to Simmek, who would be standing on the steps. He would wink to Simmek, the signal for him to begin to sing:

Der yold is mich mekaneh
Oif mein shtikele broit
Er vill fun gornit wiessen
As ich ver oisgeriessen
Az ganvenen iz bitter vie die toit.

(The "yold" is jealous of me
Of my little piece of bread
He doesn't want to know
That I'm persecuted and oppressed
And that stealing is more bitter than death.)

Simmek sang so beautifully that soon a large crowd would assemble standing with mouths agape, eyes tearful. Simmek sang song after song, in Yiddish, Polish, and Russian. When the secret session of the underground was over, Zlotovitz would stick out his head. The "concert" would conclude, and the audience would disperse. "Harish (a pet name for Hirsch) was my idol," Simmek declared proudly of his brother. "Since my childhood I wanted to be like him. When Harish returned from the forest to the work camp in order to get us out, we embraced with unrestrained joy. Then standing for a moment he smiled secretly, tousled my hair, and said, 'Didn't I tell you I would come back?'

"Harish's return to the camp caused a tempest. At dusk

151

the active members of the underground meet to begin plans for our getaway. I was lying on a bed in the corner, pretending to be asleep. I listened to what soon became heated arguments, for there were some who accused my brother of endangering our lives. They demanded that he leave the camp. Harish begged them to reconsider and to concentrate on the escape itself. Most of the group sided with Harish, and I felt a sudden surge of excitement and anticipation.

"That night we left Sverzhna, running through the snow. There were shots. We ran frantically from the camp, not slowing down until the light of dawn when we found ourselves outside a village. My brother mustered a few sleighs and seated only the exhausted. He turned to me, man to man, and said, 'It's clear that we two are in command, so we will go on on foot.'

"Harish always treated me as an adult. I remember that after we reached the partisan camp, he left for the Kopyl region to search for weapons, promising to be back within a few days. Before he left, he turned to me and said, 'Take care of our sister, Henya. Now, you are the man in the family.' I responded with a nod. He then bent down and took a copper spoon out of his boot. With a spoon in your hand, you were able to 'catch' a bit of soup, some *balanda*. With it, you would never go hungry, without one, you weren't even in the game. He threw the spoon toward me and said, 'Take care of it until I return.' I took care of the spoon until I learned that he had been murdered by the Russian Anentchenko."

Simmek had a secret side in which no one else could take part. He had his daydreams: he would grow up to be like his brother; he would return to the town of his childhood. His maturity did not totally erase the child within. Once he took a stick, attached a rag to it, and constructed a flag. He waved the flag about and then thrust the stick into the fire so the end became red hot. "Look! Look! I can turn the world into a heap of ruins. He then set the heated end of the stick against the bark of a tree and called out: "This is my marker so I may come back after the war." He wrote, "Here I lived in the year 1943—I, Simmek, age 9."

Simmek learned how to give shaves in the forest. "One day," he related, "an old Jew, *Menaker,* came to me in a camp, waving a half-broken instrument in his hand. Pointing at his beard he said, 'Simmek, shneid arum, ya, pavolye, pavolye. Ich hob tseit.' ('Cut around, yes, slowly, slowly. I have time.') He handed me the instrument, a razor with its cutting edge eaten away except for an end section left intact to shave with. Menaker seated himself by a tree and said, 'vart a minut' ('wait a minute'), then releasing one great glob of spit, prepared himself for the 'barber.' This was the first time I had held a razor in my hand, but I began to work.

"Suddenly my hand slipped and the razor got stuck in my customer's nose. Menaker jumped up as if he had been bitten by a snake and cried out, 'Er hot mir avekgeharget!' ('He's killed me!') and kicked my ass. After that I was always the camp barber!"

One day, Nikulski, the commander of the parachutists, was sitting prepared for his shave, with his gun between his knees. He said in a jesting tone to Simmek, "If you cut my throat with the razor, I'll shoot you." Simmek shot back to him, "After I cut your throat, you'll be permitted to shoot me, but not before!"

One day, a handful of children in the forest planned an "ambush" of Nikulski's men. They lay in wait, checking the partisans' activities, when they would set out, when they would return. They scouted along the trails in the vicinity of the camp and planned their attack. It was a winter day. They piled great mounds of snow and prepared snow forts. They identified positions where they could take cover and establish a second line of defense. The "mission" was to attack Nikulski and his group with snow balls as they were returning from an operation. In the middle of these preparations, the children suddenly heard Henya's voice coming from the camp. "Simmek, come quickly to the tent, I have to wash your pants, and I finally have hot water." The "commander" of the ambush had to retreat from the battle area, head down, face red.

"She always spoils the *Zassadas* ("ambushes")," Simmek mumbled to himself. "How can you talk to me of washing my pants, me, a brigade commander . . ."

Much later, Yehuda and Levi Neufeld came to the forest. Yehuda was about ten, Levi, seven. I had known the two children from Nesvizh before the outbreak of the war. For a while I had done carpentry work with their father in the ghetto, and both of us used to go to the Radzivil palace to repair closets and tables. During the last days of the ghetto, especially after the annihilation of the Horodzei ghetto, there was a prevading anxious feeling. Neufeld, the father, came to me and asked for advice. Should he send his children off to Zobovitz, the gentile cobbler, who lived not far from our house? I knew Zobovitz to be a good and honest man, and I replied that he should send them without delay.

On July 19, 1942, we stood near the wire fence facing the cemetery a few meters from my house, mother and father Neufeld, Yehuda, Levi, and myself. It was dusk and the streets were empty. The light rain had finally stopped. Before us stretched a dirt road, and beyond were the straw-roofed barns of the local peasants. The parents kissed their children. Eyes filled with tears. The children looked at them in sadness and silence. We lifted the wires and the children slipped underneath, setting out, alone, barefoot. They looked back once. We followed them for about two hundred meters, the fence between us, until they turned and disappeared from our sight. We stood tensely. Would they arrive safely? Would we see them again? We didn't hear any cries or shooting, so after a long silence, we turned and walked back to the ghetto. The children passed Albyenska, Pilsudskigo, and then reached the home of Zobovitz.

"Zobovitz received us warmly," Yehuda told us. "We ate in their house and slept in the barn. The next day the ghetto was in flames. Zobovitz consoled us, suggesting that our parents might have fled to the forest.

"The three daughters in the house cared for us as kindly as their parents did. The food was good. What they ate, we ate. The days were long, the nights even longer. We had nothing to do. We didn't know what to do with ourselves. I already knew how to read, Levi did not. I read all the books in the house.

"We used to receive the Belorussian newspapers, which were full of war news. Zobovitz knew the Russians were advancing and told us, giving us hope. They sewed warm clothes for us and supplied us with blankets. But despite all that was provided, we were not to be comforted. There was always that fear. Each knock at the door terrified us.

"When the search for Jews became more intense, Zobovitz had a relative from a neighboring village bring a cart. We were placed in it and covered with straw. The peasant drove us off. We were transported to a barn several kilometers away. We hid in the barn for twenty-four hours, and on the following day, another peasant came and brought us to the partisans in the forest."

The family camp to which Yehuda and Levi had come was commanded by Avraham Weinberg, and it belonged to our unit, the Zhukov unit. Henka and Avraham Weinberg prepared a tent of reeds and straw for the children. Though they were sad, the children retained that certain look in their eyes—the noble look that comes from suffering. Gentle, quiet, and well behaved, they gradually found their place in the forest. Levi learned to read and write, and both of them studied geography and arithmetic.

155

Left to right: Yitzhak Zuckerman, Abba Kovner, and Shalom Cholawski, at the unveiling of the Ghetto Monument, Warsaw, April 1948.

View of Nesvizh.

City Hall at Market Square.

The Bridge over the lake in the "New City" with the Slutzk Gate in the background.

Courtyard of the Radzivil Palace.

Pilsudski Street where the author's home once stood.

Yehuda would bring back the *svodka* ("war communique") from the nearby staff command. Becoming proficient in Russian, he would read the news to the older folks, explaining the geographical locations of the cities the Red Army had liberated. At times, he would add his own political commentary.

Levi and Yehuda were never a burden even in difficult times. They were extremely independent and never allowed themselves to be pampered. Whatever suffering they did was in silence.

The summer months of 1943 were a disappointment for us. Russian victories cheered us, but the great hope that the collapse of the German army was close remained unfulfilled. The Red Army advanced at a snail's pace, and the German army consistently mounted counterattacks. The mood in the unit was also one of discouragement. The strained relationships that emerged during the tense period of trouble and wandering had left deep scars. Only among the Jews did the sense of fraternity increase. When mixed groups of partisans went out on missions, the Jewish fighter, feeling a Jewish comrade at his side, knew he could rely on his support in time of trouble.

Once while scouting abandoned houses I spotted a book of letters by Maxim Gorky. As I turned its pages by the light of burning splinters in the dead of the night, I found Gorky's article on Bialik. I tore the two pages out of the book and brought them to the unit. As the group sat together that night, I took the pages out of my pocket and read them. What spirit! How much encouragement and strength these pages brought us! The men sat transfixed; even the Russian Jews, some of whom had never heard of Bialik, absorbed the lines with open hearts. Even the poor Russian translation did not diminish the intensity of Bialik's verse:

Hangman! Here's the neck—rise and strike
Behead me like a dog—you've an arm with an axe,
While all the earth is my block—
And we—we are the few!
My blood is allowed, strike a skull and let the blood flow,
Blood of suckling and greybeard—and spurt on your shirt—
And it will not be erased for eternity!

We found the following lines from Heine's "Intermezzo":

There stands a lonely pine tree
In the north, on a barren height.

Of all the remnants of religious and cultural life that we chanced to come upon in our reconnaisance missions, none was more valuable than an illustrated parchment we found torn from a *Torah* scroll. When the parchment was brought back to the unit, the coarse hands of the Jewish fighters fondled it tearfully. Years afterwards, as a witness at the Eichmann trial, I brought the parchment as evidence before the judges.

Once, after a Russian plane had dropped guns, ammunition, and recent newspapers by parachute, a copy of *Izvestiya* came into my hands, and I spotted an article entitled "Our Humanism" by Ilya Ehrenburg. I had known of Ehrenburg even in my youth when I read his "Hulio Huranito," "13 Pipes", and "Dream Factory". He was a fascinating talent who, at the outbreak of Nazism in Germany, turned his pen against the mighty enemy. Each one of his articles contained spiritual nourishment for the soldier at the front and the partisan in the forest. This article in *Izvestiya* was brilliantly written, uncovering the baseness of Western culture and stripping the logic of the so-called great human truth promoted by Nazi Germany. The closing sentence is one I will never forget: "We are bearing humanism—our humanism—on the tips of bayonets." After the war, in Ehrenburg's *Book of Letters* compiled from the thousands of letters he received from soldiers at the front, there was the following brief letter:

Dear Ehrenburg!
    I should like to send you something precious as a remembrance, but what can a soldier at the front send you? I have to my credit thirty-six dead enemies. I shall send you half. To your credit I transfer eighteen fallen German soldiers!

In the beginning of September 1943, Polish units received orders to hit Russian and Jewish partisan units. We were now waging war against the Poles and the Germans, and it was not long before fighters in our brigade had an encounter with the new enemy. Harkavi and his group, while on an operation in the Naliboki region, were attacked by a band of armed Poles. The Jewish fighting men fought bravely until the last bullet, but among those who fell were Yosef Harkavi, Boaz Axelrod, Moishele Weinstein, and Atman and Sheneour Bernstein. The news of the battle and the Polish betrayal spread quickly through the Naliboki forests.

Another group of men, among them Binyamin Vilitovski, Yitzhak Perzovitz, and Shmuel Nissenbaum, set out toward Sverzhna to blow up the sawmill at the work camp. The partisans succeeded in entering the mill and lighting the explosives, but a guard discovered the fire and extinguished it as the group left. Little damage was done.

In a sabotage operation in the Kopyl region, brave Fela Weinberg fell. She was a refugee from Warsaw, young and daring, frequently volunteering to undertake difficult missions. After successfully establishing contacts in the town of Slutsk, she volunteered to blow up the local electrical power station. Reconnoitering near the town, Fela felt that she had aroused the suspicion of a villager, so she withdrew. Armed with a new plan, and hiding the explosives in a large loaf of bread, she once again set out on her mission. She never returned. We later learned that she had been caught in Slutzk and hanged in the square.

As Jewish brotherhood increased, fierce competition arose between the Jewish and Russian fighters, each group volunteering to top the other in acts of sabotage and in battle.

With the coming of fall, the Jewish unit moved to Ruzhani in the Kletsk region. Cold weather forced the unit to move closer to the marsh area, which would provide a safe haven in case retreat became necessary. Our mission was to sabotage telephone communications and secondary roads in the area of the Moscow-Warsaw highway. Stregelski, Rozen, and I went on these missions with a group of fighting men from various companies. Initially, we were successful, but then the Germans began to outwit us, and we paid in blood. The Germans concealed mines close to the telephone posts, but the partisans caught on to this and devised a system of detection. We avoided injury until the enemy hid mines in the poles themselves. Kadashitz and Ya'akov Peres were severely wounded by such mines, and both later died of these wounds.

One November night, a group was organized under the command of Byalousov to acquire food. As we entered a village, we were suspicious because it was too quiet. When we found no one in the first houses, we began advancing toward the main square. We had barely gone a hundred meters when we were hit by fire. The group ran to safety in the darkness of the woods, but discovered that two of our men were missing. The next day one returned with the news that the other had been mortally wounded. The Germans had hidden his body in the village graveyard.

We retaliated a few days later. Binyamin Vilitovski, one of our "sappers," set out with four men to burn the bridge near

163

Ozda. Ordinarily, this mission would never have been undertaken because the police always kept a strict watch at the bridge. But Velitovski and his men spent several days gathering information, especially on the changing of the guard. They learned, by chance, that one of the guards at the bridge was to be married the next day. They assumed that the police would be drunk and the guard limited. The next evening, Velitovski and his men crawled close to the bridge, each one bearing a sheaf of straw. They set the bundles on the side of the bridge and ignited them. As the guards opened fire, the bridge burst into flames. Vilitovski and his group returned to Ruzhani in triumph.

The Germans, with the help of the police at Zaustrovitz, set up a number of ambushes in Moritz. Prudence and alertness as well as familiarity with the area saved the partisans from falling into their traps, but too often there were casualties.

On one mission, we were to pass through the Hominka region near Zaustrovitz. In the marsh area, we had to lay a wooden road, splitting logs lengthwise to make the roadway. As we were working at this, our scouts on horses advanced to reconnoiter. When they got to the edge of the forest, they entered a rain of bullets. Only by a miracle, and by their great agility, were Mishke Neimark and Hanan, the two expert and daring Jewish scouts, saved. Both were nineteen years old. Mishke Neimark had his horse shot out from under him, but without regard for his life, he removed the harness from the horse while still under fire and returned with it to the unit.

The Germans, led by the local police, were persistent. They dicovered the location of the unit's defense post near the burned-out village of Kolki and encircled it, cutting off the road leading to the unit. Paula Lip was caught in this maneuver, and the enemy tortured and executed her.

During this period, the partisans, operating through the underground, managed to establish contact with the

Zaustrovitz police. As a result, five police joined the Jewish unit. Two of them, Tsahan and Zhukovski, joined my platoon, and I kept a close watch on them. It was quite probable that they had taken an active part in the Hominka ambush in which eight partisans were killed, among them five Jews. It was no easy thing to tolerate these former police in the unit, though they categorically denied any wrongdoing. The excuse was that the police had been recruited against their will by the Germans, and the command was forced to accept them.

At the close of winter, the command decided that it was no longer necessary to base the Jewish unit in the Ruzhani district, so we were ordered to pull up stakes. We subsequently roamed the forests for weeks. The nights were our time for patrolling, carrying out operations, and moving on. During these long, wet, spring nights, we encountered forest, darkness, rain. When an occasional glimmer of light appeared at the edge of a forest, it was life itself revealed in the wilderness. We would drag ourselves toward the beacon, sometimes too weary to fear danger.

More than a nuisance on these nighttime missions were the guard dogs at peasants' houses. The barking of just one dog inevitably attracted all the other dogs in the neighborhood and this in turn signalled the informers and collaborators that partisans were around. Many a fighter paid with his life because of these dogs.

We longed to enter a warm home and nourish the stomach and the heart. It was indeed a rare moment to be welcomed in by a peasant and be wondrously overcome by the gentle smell of home cooked food:

The peasant is sitting comfortably at the head of the table, where rests in the middle, a heap of fresh, warm meal-pancakes. Like a proper guest invited to dine, you take a seat, tear a pancake into little pieces and dip them one by one into a pan bubbling hot with bits of meat and fat. The little boy sitting opposite his father says, "Daddy, there

165

are so many pancakes between you and me that I can't even see you!'' ''God willing,'' answers the father, ''next year we shall be privileged with such abundance that, once again, there will be a mountain of food before us.''

Returning from some late night act of sabotage to the blue sky of morning, we would jump off our sleighs and fill up our canteens at a peasant's house. When our canteens were full with liquor called *samigon,* our spirits would run high, and our horses would gallop with renewed energy toward the forest in the distance.

Our meetings with the Baptists were reminders of kindness and admiration. They were a religious sect devoted to the Holy Bible and to the messianic mission of the Jewish people. They lived in a different spiritual world from others in the area, and their lives seemed separated from the hatred and murder that surrounded them. The partisans usually aroused respect in the local population, respect for their strength and their weapons. But with the Baptists, it was different. For them, the human being came first. They showed respect toward Jews and our ideals, and they made us feel that it was a privilege for them to be our hosts. Their compassion aroused deep feelings among the Jewish fighters. They provided a refuge and sanctuary for human values.

Unfortunately, acts of kindness from villagers were less common than hostile actions. On some occasions, our controlled rage against unfriendly peasants suddenly burst forth. The command always regarded these cases with severity and, at times, meted out heavy punishment to those who harmed or offended peasants. Sometimes partisan groups had to restrain their own members to keep them out of trouble. Mishke Niemark was one of those who needed to be held in check for his own good.

Mishke was in the same platoon with Feivel Tunik. Before the war, he was a *gavnovoz* (''lavatory janitor'') at the Badizi Kolkhoz near Kopyl, but he knew his job as a partisan. He was an expert gunner, and his appearance and manner of talk put the fear of God into the population. Tall, powerfully built, with huge lips, he would follow every sentence with *k'ebani ma'at* ("Go----your mother"). Needless to say, we received many complaints about him. The commander warned him that if he did not improve his behavior toward the local population, he would be shot. Mishke promised that in the future he would behave accordingly.

A few days later, he was sent out on a mission with Feivel and a few partisans. It was a hazy night, and they were not familiar with the road. Deciding to ask directions at a nearby house, Mishke was the first to jump the fence and knock on the window. His comrades had tried to hold him back saying it was best to send someone else. Mishke might break the glass when he knocked. "Let me do it, comrades. You'll see that I will behave very nicely to the peasants," Mishke begged. His comrades consented, but warned him most severely to guard his tongue. "You can rely on me. You will see how I've changed."

At Mishke's gentle knock, a peasant woman opened the door, and Mishke turned toward her, bowed, and most politely said, "Zdravstvi tchiotka, tak ti nia bossya k'ebani ma'at . . ." ("How do you do, auntie. Don't be afraid, k'ebani ma'at . . ."). The partisans returning from the mission told this story to the enjoyment of the unit, and Mishke got a new nickname, "Zdravstvi tchiotka, k'ebani ma'at!"

From the end of 1943 until liberation, Soviet authority prevailed in the forest. It watched the partisans carefully, and the men in the unit were less free to speak out than they had been. A Soviet circular served to educate and train the citizens in the region and to fight German propaganda. A press was set up at Ruzhani to serve the Kleck region. Weiner was in charge, and he chose Yoel Mazorovitz as his assistant, Shalom Katchanovski as the radio man, and Yarotski as editorial assistant. Weiner acquired the printing materials at Vizna, and Yoel was drafted to work the press. A weekly newspaper appeared containing news from the front, as relayed by radio and through memos. This team of workers remained at Ruzhani until liberation.

In our nocturnal visits to the homes of peasants, we retold reports of the murderous nature of the German regime. The peasants, along with their wives and children, listened intently to our words. We brought triumphant news from the front and would tell of the actions of the Germans in the neighboring villages. At times, I would quote Ehrenburg. When I spoke to them in their native language, the peasants would accept us as true liberators and friends.

In November 1943, the Red Army crossed the Dnieper. Kiev was taken the same month, and the expanses of the Ukraine and White Russia were laid open before the Red Army. The advance of the army was slow, but it proceeded unyielding. During January and February of 1944, the Red Army reached Rovno, Sarni, and Kovel in a penetration that became the famous "Vatutin's Sword." The front, for the partisans of Polesye, lay to the east as well as the south, and extended along the boundary between Polesye and Wohlinia.

With the advance of the Red Army, the partisan movement had to redefine its strategy. Some of the units, among them Kapusta's, were sent to strike against the fleeing enemy. Other units remained within the districts to establish an underground authority, to surface victoriously with the coming of the Red Army. This would relieve the Army of having first to garrison the districts and then, subsequently, to transfer administrative personnel to strengthen and guard the liberated areas. The partisan unit assigned to a certain area would have to be well informed of those who could be trusted in the villages. As the Red Army drew closer, however, Soviet authority penetrated deeper and deeper into the structure of each partisan unit and political party affiliation became more and more important.

An airfield was set up near Ruzhani. The route to Moscow was tightened. Some German prisoners were transported by plane for interrogation; others remained in the forest.

I was sent by Baranov to the Tsihomirov unit to act as an interpreter during the interrogation of German prisoners. When the prisoners learned they had fallen into the hands of partisans, they were frantic. Horror stories of the cruelty of the partisans had passed among the Germans. The director of the Tsihomirov "special platoon" took the prisoners to a camp. There they were well fed, and the guards were kept well in the background. The director shrewdly understood that these soldiers had little to tell, but if they were assured lenient treatment, they might give us a picture of their way of life and the general mood of the German army. The prisoners began talking about their families, about the gift parcels of chocolate, dried fruits, and juices they received, and finally of army conditions.

They soon became so relaxed that they began to tell jokes. I remember one of them telling a revealing story that had Goering, Goebbels, and Hitler called up before God to be judged. The Creator asked Goering, "How many times did you lie to the people of the world?" "Seven times" was Goering's answer. God immediately passed judgment. Goering was sentenced to run seven times around heaven. "March!" said the Lord. "And you, Goebbels?" "I lied twenty times." "Twenty times around Heaven. March!" said the Lord. Then it was Hitler's turn. He approached God and said, "Look, Lord, I know what you're going to ask, so how about a motorcycle? Running around heaven forever will be murder on my feet!"

The prisoners laughed riotously. When they were asked, "Are you ready to fight against Hitler?" they answered,

169

"Against Hitler, yes! But not against Germans!" We promised to transport them by plane to Moscow so they could join up with General Paulus. They believed this and were happy. The next day they were transported not to Moscow, but to the world beyond.

At the end of February 1944, we received instructions from division command to attach ourselves to a new brigade, the nineteenth, which was being organized from various units—the Molotov, Zhukov, Lazo, and Grizodublov units. Relieved to give up our nomadic life of the past year, we gladly joined the march back to Svititza in the marshes of northern Polesye. Once there the new brigade was to clean the forest of spies, cement partisan relationships with the population, and hold the area until liberation. On the march, Yitzhak Perzovitz, one of the youngest and most courageous partisans in the Jewish unit, was killed in a skirmish.

In the Mashuki forests on the way to Polesye, the brigade was reunited with the Jewish family camp headed by Eliezer Segal. It had grown, absorbing Jews who had escaped from German work camps as well as Belorussians and village contacts afraid of reprisals. When the Molotov, Zhukov, Lazo, and Grizodublov units regrouped to form the new brigade, an agreement was struck that now directly affected the fortunes of the family camp. According to the verbal agreement, each unit was responsible for its own, and each was obligated to provide one cow each week to the family camp. Soon after the reunion with the family group, a bakery was set up in the family camp, and each unit of the brigade ws allowed to bake bread there using its own flour. Thus, by combining a few contributions with its own skill and know-how, the family camp came to live quite respectably.

At the end of March, I went with Yosef Pecker, Ginsberg, and a few others to the Lipniki area. There, in the depths of

170

Polesye units of the Komarov division were cramped. Along the road, stretched tremendous marsh areas interrupted occasionally by withered, impoverished villages of Polesye. Here was poverty such as we had never seen. Not a drop of milk for the children, no bread, no potatoes. It was difficult to comprehend how people could live in such conditions. At times we met people eating *makucha,* the remains from oil seeds ordinarily used for animal feed. Before the war these peasants had exited by herding and trading cattle. Each peasant, even the poorest, raised twenty to thirty head, and their oxen were large and fat. But now the cattle supply had been reduced drastically by the Germans and the partisans, and two or three families were forced to share a single cow. In the spring of 1944, these families were famished. Life in the villages was at a standstill. Polesye was mournful and desolate.

Savititza, in the marshes of Polesye, was a burnt out village. Its inhabitants dwelt in earthen huts in the marsh under the protection of the partisans. The marshes were full of rot and stench; only here and there did a dry patch crop up. The few paths were made of logs, roots, and scattered broken branches.

The ability of the inhabitant of Polesye to adapt himself to the region amazed us. To follow the tracks of these men through the marshes and forests was to be astonished by their ability to traverse dangerous swamp lands quickly. These peasants were extraordinarily agile, and they had a natural instinct, like that of an animal, for utilizing and balancing the body however treacherous the footing. With measured movements, with a minimum of effort, and without a moment of hesitation, they were able to cross the wet, soft land. Fitted with highly flexible *laptches,* which were shoes knitted from the bark of trees, native trackers rarely even wet their feet in the mud, much less sink into it. They knew every sign and secret of the marsh—where moss was abundant, where certain kinds of trees grew, and the locations of birds' nests. Every natural setting opened before the local tracker like a book. He was able to enter a thick forest that had no path or road, journey through it for hours, and reappear at the same point at which he entered. In the beginning, the partisans had made use of the local trackers to find their way around the area.

With the advance of spring, however, the waters increased and the plague of mosquitoes became unbearable. Even the natives of Polesye refused to enter the marsh. The mosquitoes swarmed like locusts. It seemed to us that every cubic centimeter of space was filled by a mosquito. They were a giant species. You could watch a mosquito land on your arm and calmly bloat its belly with your blood like a car filling up at a gas pump. Even when you curled up and covered yourself with your army blanket, careful not to leave any space open, they would still get at you.

We had an epidemic of boils in the unit, and the crowded conditions in the earthen huts added to its inevitable spread. There was no remedy. When the boils burst, the shirt stuck to the open wounds. It was impossible to lie down, because they covered your back, your chest, and your arms.

Along with the mosquitoes and boils, came typhus. As soon as a case was diagnosed, that person was quarantined. But medicine was scarce. Antonenko, a medical student who served as the unit doctor, used various leaves and dried blackberries as a poultice. Nature did not coddle us, and the men somehow accustomed themselves to conditions.

We overcame each burden until another obstacle was hurled at us. The Zhurkintses, a gang of partisans whose principle enjoyment was the murder of Jews, began terrorizing the area, ravaging and murdering. They attacked peasants living in the forest, stealing their horses and whatever remained of their possessions; gifts of vodka would sometimes appease them.

A company of Jews from Baranovichi and Slonim had camped near the Vignovi Lake. At their disposal were some weapons, which had been acquired through many sacrifices. The Zhurkintses robbed them of their weapons and killed most of them. Many Jewish groups that had escaped from the areas north of the marshes of Polesye were annihilated by these outlaws.

The commander of the Zhurkintses was called before Orlovski and ordered to leave the area and to return all the stolen weapons. After this warning the murderous band disappeared, cropping up only occasionally to attack swiftly and then retreat again into hiding.

In the spring of 1944, the brutality of the Germans toward the local population forced many of the villagers to make their way to the partisan camps. These last minute patriots comprised most of the Grizodubov unit. They brought their families and their sheep, cattle, and wealth. They built large, roomy, earthen huts. They were optimistic, cheerful and helpful, and their allegiance earned them the right to be called partisans, fighers for the liberation of the homeland.

With this exodus to the forest came many German spies. In the two years we spent in the forests, there were never as many spies as during those last months. They were part of a last ditch effort by the Germans to ease the retreat of their army by stepping up intelligence activities. Women played an important part in the scheme. When they arrived at the camp, they quickly befriended partisans. We were in a continual state of tension, anxious to uncover the spies and prevent them from carrying out their assignments.

A comrade of ours, the Jewish partisan Olivenstein, who had come to the forest from the Nesvizh ghetto, joined a mission to a nearby village near the Moscow-Warsaw road. One shrewd German spy alerted the police, and in the clash that night between police and partisans, Olivenstein fell. He had been a valiant partisan during the Orliki period, but he was wounded in the back and forced to spend months recuperating. Then, on the eve of liberation, Olivenstein met death at the hands of a German spy.

The Germans began to retreat. Because we were situated near the Moscow-Warsaw road and the Stschara River, we were ordered to lay mines and plan minor skirmishes. Our location was to serve as a defense line against the Germans along the left bank of the river. For this we needed weapons, ammunition, and explosives. We received instructions from the high command to cross the front and bring equipment and ammunition from beyond the lines. The front lay west of Polesye. Sixty men from the Zhukov, Lazo, and Grizodubov units set out. Among them were Shmuel Nissenbaum and Stoklitski. After they had progressed 120 kilometers, Stoklitski came down with typhus, and Nissenbaum was ordered to bring him back to the camp. He transported Stoklitski five long days through forests and marshes until they arrived at Svititza. Meanwhile, the rest of the group crossed the front lines and returned at the end of April with automatic guns, antitank weapons, explosives, and ammunition.

We began to carry out military operations on a larger scale. The brigade command issued quotas to the partisan units for acts of sabotage and ambushes. One day in May about forty fighters from the unit went out to stage an ambush near Kriboshin off the Moscow-Warsaw road. A few moments after we set the mines a Belorussian police unit came along, singing,

Over peaks and across plains
We will march.
Jews and Communists
We will destroy.

We initiated our ambush, killing most of them with one smashing blow. But several lorries filled with enemy soldiers came up quickly from the rear, and we were forced to retreat. There were no casualties on our side.

One squad in the First Company was ordered to mine the railroads. Under similar orders, I went out in command of a group of veteran fighters and sappers to the Baranovichi district. The group included Shmuel Nissenbaum, Binyamin Velitovski, and a Russian to help us gather information from the hostile population. We took with us a sufficient amount of explosives.

The approach to the railroads at the time had become difficult because the Germans had reinforced the watch, especially along those lines that were vital for their retreat. With the assistance of local peasants who served as guides, we were able to reconnoiter the area. Between Baranovichi and the Zalanaya Station, we mined the tracks and derailed two enemy trains. We also sabotaged the telephone lines and the German stockpiles in the area. When we returned to our main base, Baranov, the Commander of the unit, gave us a special citation for the successful mission.

A few days later, on the eve of the Great Offensive along the Belorussian front, our unit set out together with the entire brigade to sabotage all the railroad lines within the partisan-controlled region. Designated "The Battle for the Railway Lines," the plan called for every partisan brigade in the area to camp beside a different section of track and to plant mines. Our section stretched along five kilometers of track. The Germans sat in fortified bunkers alongside the track and their guards kept watch between each pair of bunkers. Like all the partisan units, we bypassed the German bunkers and quickly mined the section of the track assigned to us. Somehow the Germans detected our presence and began shooting. We ran to safety, but Shalom Katchahovski, under enemy fire, first completed mining the section assigned to the neighboring Lazo unit. As we retreated some hundred meters from the tracks, a long chain of explosions flashed behind us—mission accomplished.

175

On June 23, 1944, the Great Offensive began on the Belorussian and Baltic fronts. The plan was to encircle the Germans in small pockets and prevent them from concentrating their forces and setting up a line of defense.

Minsk had been liberated on June 3, and large forces of the Red Army were diverted from Minsk to Baranovichi in the direction of Bialystok and Warsaw. The partisans coordinated certain military and civil moves with the Red Army in preparation for the offensive. A high ranking officer from the Red Army took over the command of the brigade, and army scouts reconnoitered the area with our units. This cooperation between the partisans and the Red Army strengthened as the offensive grew. Large forces of the Red Army turned toward the bridge over the Stschara River near where our forces were located. Baranovichi was bombed nightly by Red Army planes. The rumblings from the front echoed nearer and nearer from hour to hour. Then it was announced that the brigade command, as a supporting arm of the Red Army, was to undertake an important military task—to hold the bridge spanning the Stschara River.

Armed only with partisan weapons, we took our stand at the bottleneck of the main line of retreat of the German army. After the last German night patrol, units of our partisan brigade took position on the left bank of the Stschara River. At dawn, we opened fire. Our trench positions offered us defensive superiority, and we inflicted heavy losses on the German infantry. But within a short time, German tanks broke through to the bridge, and we were unable to hold out. We retreated.

Later that day we received a new assignment. South of this central bridge and several kilometers away stood the concrete pillars of a bridge that had been burned out. We hurriedly constructed a make-shift bridge on the pillars, and during the night, large numbers of Red Army infantry crossed over with light artillery. By establishing themselves in this flank position, the central bridge on the Moscow-Warsaw road was easily captured. The few German forces still remaining on the eastern side soon felt the final Russian blow.

The next day Red Army tanks entered the forest near our base. Jewish partisans met victorious Red Army soldiers, but the tremendous wave of joy that flooded the heart could not remove the feeling of deep sadness: if only they had come two years earlier! Now that the day of liberation was here, there was no one left to free.

We stood at attention to view the final military parade in the forest. For the last time, the calls of the fighters would echo through the trees. We found it hard to accept the fact that we were to leave the forests. The sufferings, dangers, and battles that we had experienced in the forests now bound us to these dark masses. The forests had once terrified us, but now they blessed us with the feeling of security. We had spent two years less two weeks in the forest—more than seven hundred days and nights! Here in the forest, hope still whispered; the outside promised uncertainty and loneliness. It seemed that once again I was being forced to flee from my home.

And yet there was life outside. There were homes that rang with the laughter of children and offered comfort and love. Would it be possible to become part of that world again?

We left the forest on July 12, 1944—a Jewish partisan unit named Zhukov. Our flag did not wave in the breeze though it fluttered in every heart. On a golden summer day, between fields of ripening corn, we walked forward. The forest gradually fell back into the distance; I paused to look back. Near the small woods and hills, clusters of Red Army men prepared for the crushing assault on the city of Baranovichi. From the edge of a wood came an elderly looking Russian officer, who, with a voice choked with joyful tears, cried out, "Yidden, partisaner!" He embraced us in true camaraderie.

Our unit approached Lakhovitz. We passed through the streets of what had once been a Jewish town. A sad wind moaned through the empty, silent houses. There were no open arms to greet us. The few who had survived hid in their homes, peering through the windows with looks of suspicion.

The unit took up temporary quarters in the churchyard at the other end of town. We hardly had a chance to change our shirts and wash when, on the following day, we were told that the Red Army was recruiting men. A corporal arrived from the command with instructions to the men in the courtyard, "Give me Jews for recruitment." Those Jewish fighters who were recruited were sent to the front, many of them to clear mine fields. Few came back.

Following the disbanding of our unit I turned toward Nesvizh.

Forest boots on my feet, my weapon resting on my shoulder, my hand grasping the barrel, I march into the city. It is Sunday, the morning of a summer's day. As I approach the quiet lake, I am once more thrilled by its stillness and beauty. It has remained untouched. Nothing has changed. I can jump once more into its waters as I did in my childhood.

Through the gate of the "New Town," I stride toward the street where my house once stood. I march along the newly paved sidewalk and turn left onto a clean street strung with lovely houses. Crowds of fresh faces, young couples and old, are walking toward me on the opposite pavement. They are heading for church. I continue walking, uneasy that perhaps I am the one heading in the wrong direction. I feel isolated, confronted. I want to scream "once I was not alone . . . I had a past, a family, my own generation . . ." As if some hand is directing me, I move on, silently.

Many eyes stare at me. They pierce my face like needles. I hear whispers of recognition: "Could he be alive?" "Yitzhak's son?" "The teacher?" "A partisan!" "O God!" I avoid their faces.

I come to the boulevard and, at the corner, find my house

still standing. Everything as it was. For a second, I think, maybe—as it was? I run to the house. I stand before it, but no door is open, no window. Not a voice is heard. I turn away, walk to view the mass grave, the bunkers. The sound and image of the ghetto in the wake of the fire jump out at me and startle my senses. I shake my head in an effort to dissolve the memory. I return to my house. I knock on the door and hear a rustling within. My heart pounds unbearably. I open the door and stop at the threshold to see familiar objects within: the copper lamp, the buffet, the table . . .

An old woman suddenly appears from the other room, looking at me in bewilderment. I recognize her. She is our neighbor. She recognizes me and stammers something. I stroke the copper lamp, imagine the buffet is still displaying all our lovely things . . . I wait. Maybe somebody will appear. Maybe . . . if I could only have a day with them, just one day . . . I wait hoping. Then I turn and leave.

Epilog: The Children

After the war, the Kravitzes adopted Levi and Yehuda Neufeld and gave them love and devotion. In the beginning of 1947, when I was visiting Salzheim, near Frankfurt, I visited with Levi at the Kravitz's home and with Yehuda at the Youth *aliyah* Camp near Fernwald. Both had studied in Israel and excelled in school. Yehuda went on to become a chief aviation engineer in Tel Aviv.

In 1957, I received a letter from Levi. He was in Jerusalem, having arrived ten years earlier. After completing high school, he had served in the army for two years and then studied at the Hebrew University Medical School. He wrote,

> It's a pity that since your visit in Germany ten years ago there has been no correspondence at all between us and for that I am responsible . . .
>
> You will surely be surprised to meet this young man of twenty one, the child you used to carry in your arms when he was small . . .
>
> Yet, although I haven't seen you since then, I have thought about you from time to time and it seems to me there will always exist that closeness between us . . .

Shortly afterwards, Levi came to visit me at my home in Kibbutz Ein Hashofet. I was overjoyed to see him, a good looking young man, impressive in his appearance and speech. The evening he arrived there was a party at the Harei Ephraim School to celebrate the publication of *Sefer Ha-partizanim Ha-yehudim,* of which I was one of the authors. I invited Levi to come along with me. When the party was over, we spent a long time talking. I was deeply impressed by his knowledge, but shaken by his sullenness.

Some time later, I received the unhappy news that Levi had disappeared. I feared for him, hearing that he had been going through many changes. One day police officers came to my home asking about Levi. To my great amazement, they told me that Levi had been a suspect in connection with a series of murders, hence his disappearance. Despite the allegations, I repeatedly held to my conviction that Levi was honest and guiltless of these crimes. Manhunts to track Levi down proved futile.

Some months later, a young boy chanced upon Levi's body in an abandoned house in Ein Kerem near Jerusalem, the city he loved. Near him was a letter containing farewell words, asking forgiveness from his foster parents. Later the police announced that they had removed all suspicion from Levi Neufeld.

I delivered the eulogy at Levi's grave. Zelda, the poet, wrote a poem entitled "The Invisible Carmel" in his memory:

His locks flowed like a secret brook—
Like silk, like peace,
When they washed him from the clay and mud
And the darkness of the pit.
We said:
Here the sun has kissed an orphan's eyes
And now the past has been erased with infinite light.
We said:
In the warm light of this holy city

There will stand a tree to perpetuate new generations
Across the slopes and hills.
But the distant fears
The invisible ones
Lay in his bed
Drank from his cup
Touched his bread
Read his books
And dreamt his dreams—
Until they grew taller than he
And their power greater.
And the unseen fears
Set fire to the mysterious, hidden
Pattern of belonging
To the land and what it contains.
The fear consumed all,
Even the laws.
His precious body fell from him.
The lost one
Wept in the bosom of the grass,
Told the grass
How terrible was the shame of the humbled one
To meet the sun's desire
Every morning.
The grass did not urge him to live
The grass did not urge him to rise,
The grass sang
Of the soul's joy
To meet in the world to come
Its mother and father
And its Creator.

Shraga "Feodus" Filler works in a garage in Tel Aviv.
Simmek, now known as Shimon Israeli, sings professionally
in Israel. I have visited Shraga's home in Tel Aviv, Yehuda's
home in Kfar Shemaryahu, and Shimon's on the slope of the
Carmel in Haifa. I have come to know their spouses and the
children: Avi and Sara Filler; Shemuel, Oded, and Orna
Neufeld; and Ofer and Iris Israeli. I find in the faces of these
children more than a hint of resemblance to Feodus, Yehuda,
and Simmek.